TWAYNE'S WORLD AUTHORS SERIES
A Survey of the World's Literature

FRANCE

Maxwell A. Smith, Guerry Professor of French, Emeritus
The University of Chattanooga
Former Visiting Professor in Modern Languages
The Florida State University

EDITOR

Villiers de l'Isle-Adam

TWAS 491

Villiers de l'Isle-Adam

VILLIERS DE L'ISLE-ADAM

By WILLIAM T. CONROY, JR.

*Queens College of the
City University of
New York*

TWAYNE PUBLISHERS

A DIVISION OF G. K. HALL & CO., BOSTON

Library of Congress Cataloging in Publication Data

Conroy, William Thomas.
Villiers de l'Isle-Adam.

(Twayne's world authors series; TWAS 491 : France)
Bibliography: p. 159–62
Includes index.
1. Villiers de l'Isle-Adam, Jean Marie Mathias
Philippe Auguste, comte de, 1838–1889.   2. Authors,
French—19th century—Biography.
PQ2476.V4Z559   848'.8'09 [B]   78-1812
ISBN 0-8057-6332-5

For My Family

Contents

About the Author

William Thomas Conroy, Jr., is assistant professor of French and Comparative Literature at Queens College of the City University of New York. After graduation from Holy Cross College, he received a Fulbright scholarship for graduate work at the University of Clermont-Ferrand, France. Following these studies, he was awarded a Woodrow Wilson fellowship to Princeton University, where he completed his M. A. and Ph. D. degrees. Dr. Conroy is the author of *Diderot's Essai sur Sénèque* (Banbury: Voltaire Foundation, 1975), a critical study of the French philosopher's final work. In addition, he has contributed articles and reviews to various journals, including a review of an exhibition by the artist and sculptor Arman, published in *Arts Magazine* (April 1978). His translation of selections from Jean Mitry's book on director John Ford will soon appear in *Wide Angle*. Professor Conroy has recently been selected for *Who's Who in the East*.

Preface

In his later years, Villiers de l'Isle-Adam (1838–1889) enjoyed not only a certain celebrity among French readers but the reverence of contemporary writers, who hailed him as a father of French Symbolism. Yet after his death, with the eclipse of the Symbolist movement, his reputation suffered a complete reversal; by 1900, his name was no longer mentioned in literary circles. As Diderot remarked, "Nothing [is] stable in this world: today at the top, tomorrow at the bottom of the wheel."[1] Thanks to studies by E. de Rougemont (1910) and Fernand Clerget (1913) and a surge of interest in him during the 1930s, mostly from Surrealists and critics interested in Symbolism as a historical movement, as well as the recent scholarship of E. Drougard, Joseph Bollery, P.-G. Castex, and A. W. Raitt, Villiers' reputation has staged a slow but steady comeback. A production of Axël at the Champs-Elysées Theater in 1962, the first since 1894, and the premiere performance of Le Prétendant in 1965 on French television have again brought his name before the French public at large.

Despite the reflowering of his reputation in France, Villiers remains relatively unknown in the English-speaking world. Many students of literature are unacquainted with his name, let alone his works, and few critics have thought him important enough to devote time to him. With the exception of references in Arthur Symons' The Symbolist Movement in Literature (1899) and the wider treatment in Axel's Castle (1931), Edmund Wilson's study of the influence Villiers had on the next generation of writers, there is virtually nothing in English about the French conteur and dramatist.

The present book, the first comprehensive study of Villiers in English, was undertaken in hopes of redressing the neglect this seminal writer has suffered in the English-speaking world. Although primarily concerned with Villiers the writer, it does not ignore the man's life or the influence he exercised on both his contemporaries and posterity. The work has been written with two audiences in view, the general reader and the literary specialist. Consequently, synopses of works have been included for those who may be reading Villiers for the first time, and most citations have been given in English. For obvious reasons, some quotations from Villiers' poetry, some from his prose poems, and others displaying popular pronunciation have been kept in the original; translations are then provided. Information that may be interesting to the specialist but not necessarily to the general reader has been placed in the notes.

The rewards from this study have been immeasurable, but the voyage has not always been smooth. *Ad astra per aspera*. In compiling biography, one must constantly sift fact from fiction, and with Villiers this process proved no easy matter. Not only did he sometimes "drop out" of society, enveloping himself in mystery, but he also fostered myths about his life, which some biographers have too readily perpetuated. I have tried to adhere strictly to the documentary evidence. Variant readings posed another problem. Villiers was forever revising his works, and this was no less true even after he had published them. Some of the short stories, for example, exist in three or four published versions. In most cases, I have dealt with the definitive rendering not simply because it represents the best example of Villiers' art but also because it is the one reproduced and thus the most accessible to the reader. An exception has been made in two instances. Separate treatment is given to *Morgane* and its later version, *Le Prétendant*, since the difference between the two is substantial. Since Villiers' early stories play so decisive a role in his career, they are treated in their original form, with an indication of substantial changes the author later made upon them. By far the most serious problem, however, involved organization. It appeared to me that the book could be arranged either chronologically, devoting each chapter to a period of Villiers' life and works he wrote during that period, or topically, with chapters devoted to biography, poetry, novels, short prose, and theatrical works. Neither alternative, I discovered, was problem-free, but the former had the advantage of assuring a more coherent presentation, since Villiers' life and ideas of the moment so informed his writing.

It is a pleasure to acknowledge my debt to the many people who aided in the preparation of this book. Mr. Robert S. Allen of the New York Public Library has more than once put me on the track of an important discovery. Professor Byron E. Shafer of Fordham University kindly responded to an inquiry of mine concerning Villiers' biblical citations. Professor A. W. Raitt of Oxford, one of the world's leading Villierian scholars, was kind enough to answer my questions about circumstances surrounding the author's death and the publication of his posthumous works. My sincere gratitude is owed to my colleagues and friends, Professors Lucia Marino, Raymond Sayers, and John Reilly, who read portions of the manuscript and made many useful suggestions. I should also like to thank numerous friends with whom I shared thoughts on the book. Finally, I cannot forget Professor Maxwell Smith, who edited the work, and Mrs. Frances Conroy, who typed the final draft.

WILLIAM T. CONROY, JR.

Queens College of the
City University of New York

Chronology

to September, trip to Richard Wagner's home in Triebschen and to Munich.

1870 Premiere in May of *La Révolte;* from June to July, trip to Weimar, Munich, and Triebschen; outbreak in July of Franco-Prussian War; Villiers takes command of division of national guard of Paris.

1871 In March, Paris establishes its own government (Commune); Villiers contributes to newspaper *Le Tribun du peuple;* composition of *L'Evasion;* death in August of Mlle de Kérinou.

1872 Publication in October of first part of *Axël.*

1873 Publication in November of "La Découverte de M. Grave" ("L'Affichage céleste").

1873 Trip to London in December; return in January.
1874

1874 Publication of eight new tales between March and June.

1875 Villiers enters suit against directors of Châtelet Theater for playing *Perrinet Leclerc.*

1875 Publication of four new tales.
1876

1876 In January, *Le Nouveau Monde* receives prize in contest organized to celebrate the American Centennial.

1877 Publication of three new tales; Villiers begins work on *L'Eve*
1878 *future.*

1879 Increasing intimacy with Robert du Pontavice de Heussey, Villiers' biographer and Hyacinthe's son.

1880 Publication of *Le Nouveau Monde* (Richard et Cie) and first version of *L'Eve future;* beginning of liaison with Marie Dantine.

1881 In January, unsuccessful candidate for municipal council of Paris; birth of son Victor.

1882 Death in April of Villiers' mother.

1883 In February, publication of *Contes cruels* (Calmann-Lévy); premiere of *Le Nouveau Monde.*

1884 Publication in September of J.-K. Huysmans' *A Rebours;* increasing intimacy with Huysmans and Léon Bloy.

1885 Death in December of Villiers' father.

1885– Publication of revised version of *L'Eve future* and first com-
1886 plete *Axël.*

1886 Publication in March of *L'Evasion;* publication by Maurice de Brunhoff of *L'Eve future, Akëdysséril, L'Amour suprême.*

1887 Publication in May of *Tribulat Bonhomet;* premiere in October of *L'Evasion.*

1888 Publication in February of *Histoires insolites* and in November of *Nouveaux Contes cruels;* during February and March, series of lectures in Belgium; trip to Dieppe.

1889 Between April and July, stay at Nogent-sur-Marne; marriage to Marie Dantine and legitimation of Victor; death on 18 August.

1890 Posthumous publication of revised *Axël* and *Chez les passants.*

1891 Posthumous publication of *L'Evasion* in book form.

1893 Posthumous publication of *Propos d'Au-delà.*

1895 Premiere in February of *Elën.*

1901 Death on 28 April of Villiers' son Victor.

CHAPTER 1

Early Years, Early Writings

I *Breton Origins and Definitive Move to Paris (1838–1859)*

JEAN-Marie Mathias Philippe Auguste de Villiers de l'Isle-Adam
was born on 7 November 1838 in the Breton coastal town of
Saint-Brieuc into an aristocratic, yet moneyless, family. His father,
Joseph-Toussaint Charles de Villiers de l'Isle-Adam, who claimed as
ancestors both the comrade in arms of John the Fearless, Duke of
Burgundy (1371–1419), and the Grand Master of the Knights of
Malta, defender of Rhodes against the Turks (1522), not only passed
on to the boy a pride in his ancestors and a respect for religion and
the code of nobility by which they had comported themselves, but
also fired his imagination with talk of the Crusades and schemes
designed to amass unheard of treasure. Joseph-Toussaint's chief
concern in life seems to have been the restoration of the ancestral
fortune lost in the French Revolution. With this goal in mind, he
planned and plotted and ended up squandering time, energy, and
what little money he had.

The maternal side of the family provided Mathias—as young Villiers was called—with examples of greater practicality and fiscal
responsibility. His grandmother Carfort was a proverbially shrewd
Breton businesswoman and skeptical of her son-in-law's rumored
rising good fortune.[1] Mme de Carfort's maiden sister, Marie-Félix
Daniel de Kérinou, who had adopted and raised Villiers' mother,
consented—whether because she quickly intuited the elder Villiers'
disregard for practical matters or because she did not want to relin-
quish completely the company of her niece—to support the couple
and their offspring, provided that they live with her, first in Saint-
Brieuc, and after 1846 in Lannion.[2] With all her common sense,
Mlle de Kérinou could not wean Villiers' father from the chimeric

17

enterprises that were leading the family to ruin. By 1843 Joseph-Toussaint had accumulated 100,000 francs worth of debts. (At the time, Parisian masons and carpenters earned about 1100 francs per annum.) Consequently, in order to protect herself and her beloved son from this ruinous speculation and surely at the prompting of Mlle de Kérinou, Villiers' mother sought a court order restoring to the plaintiff exclusive rights over her property and preventing its seizure by her husband's creditors. The *séparation de biens* was granted on 22 August 1846.

This legal action did not stop Joseph-Toussaint, who continued to embroil Mlle de Kérinou in his exploits; nor did it bring an end to financial disputes within the family. While Villiers, like many of us, was to look back upon his childhood as a period of ideal happiness ("Good-bye then, days of childhood, oh beautiful days full of hope"[3]), the inner tension of the household left its impression on him. From these early years stemmed the contrast, observable in the adult Villiers, between a desire to forsake reality for dream and marvelous adventure, characteristic of his father, and an understanding of the practical world and a capacity in time of need to deal with it, exemplified by the maternal side of his family.

In 1847, Villiers went off to school, first to the small seminary of Tréguier, then to Saint Vincent de Paul Academy in Rennes, the *lycée* of Laval, Saint Francis Xavier Boarding School in Vannes, and finally to Saint Charles School in Saint-Brieuc. The frequency with which he changed institutions suggests that Villiers was not enraptured with studies. Perhaps the independent student chafed under the rigorous program to which his masters subjected him.[4] Perhaps his teachers were "completely insufficient for the education of this ungovernable pupil."[5] Perhaps he was distracted from study by the "divine visions of poetry" that already "hovered round him."[6] It could very well be, too, that the young boy was homesick for the house at Lannion, for his mother and great-aunt, and for the adventures of his father. In any event, after 1852, either to cure Mathias of homesickness or to take greater charge of his education, the family, always solicitous for Villiers' well-being, took up residence in Rennes, where the boy could attend classes as a day pupil. There is no evidence that Villiers pursued university studies; indeed, the difficulty he had already experienced with school would suggest that he did not.

Even though he may not have been an enthusiastic pupil, it is clear that Villiers' school years left their mark upon him. Knowledge of Hegel and Eliphas Lévi was to come only after 1859; nevertheless, an interest in philosophy, apparent in virtually all works from his first poems (1858, 1859) to *Axël* (1886, 1890), was most certainly kindled during these years. An interest in history, reflected in *Isis* (1862), *Morgane* (1866), and *Le Nouveau Monde* (1876), although probably inspired by his father's stories of ancestors and the Crusades, was nurtured by his numerous assignments in that subject.[7] Knowledge of music and an ability to play the piano, first taught by the organist at Saint-Brieuc, were developed in supplementary courses at Saint Vincent de Paul. Furthermore, Villiers' correspondence and literary pieces display the basic knowledge of Latin and antiquity he learned at school. Not only is *Isis* filled with classical references, not only do his works frequently bear epigraphs composed in Latin or drawn from Latin sources, but one letter to Baudelaire contains Villiers' French translation of a legend supposedly written in Latin (*Corr*, I, 51–53), and a part of a letter to his friend Catulle Mendès is even written in that ancient language (*Corr*, I, 151–53). It must be admitted, unfortunately, that Villiers' knowledge of the language was far from perfect and that he perhaps should have paid stricter attention to his Latin masters.[8]

Lack of documentation prevents a clear picture of what the young Villiers was like. Testimony from two fairly reliable sources, however, affords a glimpse of him during those early and adolescent days in Brittany. One of Villiers' cousins remembers young Mathias as a solitary child, who used to spend time in his room "reading, writing, napping, playing his piano" and who would sometimes "pay us the very great honor of coming down . . . and reciting to us his latest creation [*élucubration*]." One night, she continues, we had "to hear God knows what new contraption [*machine*], but the reading, I remember, this time seemed to us so ghastly, so hopelessly dull, that we were all falling asleep."[9] Apparently, the introversion this witness attributes to the boy was becoming a way of life for him. Rejection by peers, of which the incident of inattentive and dozing cousins is probably but one example, could only intensify a desire, inherited from his father, to withdraw into a world of his own creation. Yet despite this customary solitude, Louis Tiercelin claims, on the authority of his cousin Amédée Le Menant des Chesnais, a friend of Villiers, that the adolescent Mathias became successively involved with two girls. Both romances, he maintains, ended un-happily—indeed, one of them with the girl's death—and both greatly affected the youth.[10] It is conceivable that verses of the *Premières Poésies*, such as lines 46–48 of "De profundis clamavi" ("She was seventeen years old; I was scarcely that age / Often the nightingale would hold its breath / Listening to our soft steps"), line 64 of the same poem ("What then had she done to die first?" [*OC*, X, 131–32]), and lines 5–6 of "Lasciate ogni speranza" ("Farewell, you whom my voice will never awake! / Into your grave I saw my child-hood follow you" [*OC*, X, 141]), allude to one or both of these unhappy experiences and support Tiercelin's testimony.[11]

Upon completion of his studies in 1855, in order to seek glory and secure his rightful place in literary history—"We need glory. . . . When Victor Hugo is eternally snoring in his shroud of glory . . . ," he wrote cockily in late 1855 or early 1856, "I am confident I will ascend the throne . . . where he sat" (*Corr*, I, 30)—Villiers went to Paris, where he was to make several sojourns over the next three years, and where he probably first read the poetry of the Romantics.[12] There he frequented cafés and theaters, making such friends as Lemercier de Neuville, a fellow Breton and literary aspirant, and the aforementioned Amédée Le Menant. There also he published his first work, a modest, sixteen page booklet of two poems entitled *Deux Essais de poésie* (1858), and sewed "together the 5 acts of a great prose drama"—probably a first draft of *Morgane*, not published until 1866—that he was to "give, as soon as it is finished, to the Porte Saint-Martin Theater" (*Corr*, I, 31). There, too, in this "dangerous environment" (*Corr*, I, 33), to the great concern of his family, Villiers lost "the faith of his child-hood, his simple faith as a pious son of Brittany and the Church."[13]

On 9 June 1857, therefore, Villiers' father wrote to Dom Guéranger, abbot of Solesmes, asking him to "receive into your house my son" because "the solitude of the monastery and the good talks and lessons that he will have among you will lead him back to God" (*Corr*, I, 33). Villiers did not go to Solesmes, but he soon left Paris. During 1858–1859, he stayed in Montfort-sur-Meu, a small town in Brittany between Rennes and Saint-Brieuc, at the home of Amédée Le Menant des Chesnais, a young lawyer and learned Catholic whom Villiers met in Paris through his father and who sought to cure Villiers of his errors and to return him to his child-hood faith. Although there is no documentary evidence, it is plausi-ble that Amédée Le Menant prevailed upon his friend Joseph-Toussaint to let him, rather than the abbot, take charge of the youth's spiritual revitalization in a setting where "strolls" would be combined with "religious education."[14] This theory is all the more plausible since it was into Dom Guéranger's hands that Amédée Le Menant himself later recommended Villiers when he realized that the stay at Montfort had not converted Villiers into "the ardent Catholic" he "had dreamed of making."[15]

Even though the sojourn at Montfort-sur-Meu did not restore to Villiers his religious faith, it did afford him a quiet, distraction-free environment conducive to writing. According to Tiercelin, when their walks and dinner were over and Amédée had retired for the evening, "true day, that of night hours, solitude, and work, was to begin" for Villiers.[16] During these nocturnal sessions, Villiers la-bored over a series of poems that he would publish at his own expense in 1859 as *Premières Poésies*. It is certain that not all the verse contained in this collection was written at Montfort. Two poems, "Zaïra" and "Ballade," had already appeared in the *Deux Essais de poésie* (1858) and were being reprinted in the new collec-tion, the latter with a new title ("Une Façon d'imiter M. de Pom-pignan") and several revisions. Moreover, the years 1856–1858, printed on the title page of the *Premières Poésies*, tend to prove not only that "no poetry written before that first date would have been retained for the collection,"[17] but also that the work most likely contains some poems written between 1856 and 1857, prior to Vil-liers' arrival at Amédée's in 1858. Be that as it may, the poems were "largely written and gathered together at Montfort"[18], and there can be little doubt that the lines entitled "A mon ami Amédée Le Men-ant," respectfully dedicated to Villiers' host and mentor, figured among the poems written during this stay.

After the sojourn in Brittany, Villiers returned in 1859 to Paris. This time, however, his family, including Mlle de Kérinou, also came to live in the capital.[19] As a concern for Mathias' education once induced the family to take up residence in Rennes, a concern for the poet's career partially motivated the decision to move to Paris. There is little question that Villiers' parents and great-aunt were convinced of their "absolute duty to sacrifice everything in

order that the genius of the family might expand in full freedom."
They surely thought their presence would afford the financial support and material comfort necessary to assure "the final victory of
the last of the Villiers de l'Isle-Adam."[20] In all likelihood, however,
the family's concern for the young man's spiritual well-being in a
city that had already proved dangerous and a desire to watch over
him also played a part in the decision to relocate. Although Villiers
himself must have regretted the loss of complete independence that
living with his family demanded, he must have taken some comfort
in the fact that funds from Aunt Kérinou were now more accessible
and that he would no longer have to rely on the return mail to bail
him out of a tight situation.

The year of Villiers' return to Paris heralded a time of new
friends, new influences, and new directions. Gradually Villiers was
to lose contact with Amédée Le Menant and Lemercier de
Neuville,[21] as he spent more time after 1859 with his cousin
Hyacinthe du Pontavice de Heussey. That year, Pontavice introduced Villiers to the philosophical theories of Friedrich Hegel,
which were to exercise a great effect on him and whose influence is
apparent in such works as *Isis* (1862) and "Claire Lenoir" (1867). The
same year, either at Pontavice's home, or more likely at the Parisian
restaurant Brasserie des Martyrs, Villiers met Charles Baudelaire,
whom he regarded as a master and later as a friend. Not only would
the poet bring the works of Edgar Allan Poe and Richard Wagner to
his attention, but in addition, he was instrumental in Villiers' decision to abandon verse writing.

Despite encouragement from a fellow poet, Joséphin Soulary,
who claimed that "At 19 years old, you are a *good* poet; at 25, you
will certainly be a *great* poet" (*Corr*, I, 38), partially because of the
literary journals' indifference to the *Premières Poésies*,[22] more
significantly because of advice that Baudelaire surely offered him,
Villiers came to realize that "the poetic line was not his language"
and to judge his poems "with a deserved severity."[23] After the
publication of the *Premières Poésies* in 1859, therefore, Villiers
ceased writing poetry except for an occasional verse, and those he
would include in other works.[24] Henceforth, he would devote the
greater part of his time, energy, and talent to writing prose.

Not only was Villiers turning his attention to prose, but in the
same year, with the publication of two critical articles in *La
Causerie*, a "newspaper of entertainment and the coffeehouses,"[25]

he began selling his work to papers and reviews. Although remuneration was not great—Villiers, in fact, would later decry the niggardliness of editors in a story entitled "Deux Augures" (*OC*, II, 45–62; *CC*, 34–50)—his contributions over the next thirty years were to become a vital source of income for him and his family, especially after the death in 1871 of Mlle de Kérinou, heretofore the financial support of the Villiers de l'Isle-Adam. These contributions would include musical criticism and reportage ("A propos des fêtes de Bayreuth," 1876); literary criticism, such as the review of Flaubert's *Le Candidat* (1874); and most importantly, his own literary works. They would appear in such obscure and short-lived gazettes as the *Revue des Lettres et des Arts* and in such prestigious ones as the *Figaro*.

Although Villiers would forever bear the imprint of his early years in Brittany and the influence of a profligate father, a practical mother, a classical education, and unhappy adolescent loves, it is quite evident that 1859, the year of his majority, marked a turning point in Villiers' life, separating those early years (1838–1859) from what we may call the apprentice years (1860–1871). Henceforth, his life would be made not in Brittany but in Paris, where he would experience the profound influence of Pontavice and Baudelaire. Through the latter's influence, Villiers would abandon verse and establish his reputation, not as a poet, but as a prose writer. Finally, after 1859, Villiers would assume greater financial responsibility for himself and his family through his contributions to newspapers and journals.

II *Villiers as Poet*

The volume *Premières Posésie* (1859), including the revisions of two poems already published in 1858 as *Deux Essais de poésie*, contains the final version of what remains of Villiers' early writings: a collection of eight short poems, each set at night, appropriately called *Fantaisies nocturnes;* the three cantos of a long verse narrative entitled *Hermosa;* thirteen additional short poems, dealing for the most part with beginnings (morning, spring, adolescence, renaissance), grouped together under the title *Préludes;* and finally the *Chant du Calvaire*, a long work in verse, partly narrative, partly dramatic, divided into three cantos. Inasmuch as critical response to these poems has been so diverse—indifference on the part of journals immediately after their publication, hasty generalizations on

the part of many modern critics, glowing praise from Verlaine, acrid
remarks from Victor-Emile Michelet and E. de Rougemont[26]—it
would be well to reexamine their literary value.

A. *Criticism of Villiers' Poetry*

It is indisputable that much in the *Premières Poésies* (dedicated,
incidentally, to Alfred de Vigny) is derived from the Romantic poets
Villiers read as a young man. First of all, many themes found in
these poems echo those used by the Romantics. In "De profundis
clamavi" *(Préludes)*, for example, Villiers described a young man's
sorrow over the loss of a love and his nostalgic trip back to the place
where he had spent happy moments with her. This is the same
theme that Alphonse Lamartine popularized in the immortal "Le
Lac" (1820) and that Victor Hugo and Alfred de Musset later re-
worked in "Tristesse d'Olympio" (1840) and "Souvenir" (1841). The
melancholic meditation on life and death in "Barcarolle" *(Fantaisies
nocturnes)* was surely inspired by those in Lamartine's *Méditations
poétiques*. A contempt for the modern industrialized world that
Villiers expressed in such poems as "Exil" *(Fantaisies nocturnes)*
and "Découragement" *(Préludes)* was no doubt suggested by the
poetry of Vigny; in fact, the descriptions in "Exil" of Paris and
railroads ("Paris, the living furnace"; "Here the furnace roars, and
the factory toils; / In its fiery lava, the molten coal boils"; "on the
rails, the steam-engine hisses and smokes" [*OC*, X, 23]) bear a
striking resemblance to Vigny's descriptions in the poems "Paris"
published in 1831 ("the fiery Furnace"; "Everything burns, crack-
les, smokes . . . Bursts into fiery rain") and the "Maison du Berger"
of 1844 ("The thundering steam-engine"; "On the iron bull that
smokes, huffs, and bellows"). Similarly, the theme of a divinity
insensitive to the entreaties of a frail and incredulous humanity
enunciated in the *Chant du Calvaire* was borrowed from Vigny's
"Moïse" (1826) and especially from his "Mont des oliviers," first
published in 1844.

Moreover, Villiers probably took the theme of djinns and giaours,
which he used in "Chanson arabe," "Prière indienne," and "Zaïra"
(Fantaisies nocturnes), from Victor Hugo, author of *Les Orientales*
(1829), and from Lord Byron,[27] whose name Villiers mentioned in
Hermosa (*OC*,X,39) and whose *Childe Harold* he could have read in
one of the many French translations (1828, 1833, 1847, 1852). A
similarity between the Don Juan that Villiers portrayed in his *Her-*

mosa and the character developed by Musset in *Namouna* (1832)
suggests that Villiers borrowed from the latter the theme of the
disillusioned searcher of the ideal;[28] this is all the more plausible
since the epigraph to the second canto of *Hermosa* is, in fact, taken
from Musset's poem.[29] The theme of Spain, very prevalent in Villiers' early poetic works ("Une Bouteille de vin d'Espagne," "Guitare" [*Fantaisies nocturnes*], "Le Château de Seid" [*Préludes*],
Hermosa) was in all likelihood taken from the poetry of Vigny,
Hugo, Musset, and Théophile de Gautier, who were, as Professor
Hoffmann has shown, haunted by this subject.[30] Finally, it is probably more than coincidental that in the poems "Natura divina,"
"Primavera," and "Aurore" *(Préludes)*, Villiers wrote about the
fecundity and economy of nature, a theme that Gautier had developed in *Paysages* (IV, V, IX), published in 1832.

Not only did Villiers borrow themes from the Romantics he read,
he also learned from them many poetic techniques. In his poetry, he
imitated the forms (elegy, *chanson*, verse anecdote, verse narrative)
that the major French Romantics had popularized. In addition, it is
certain that Villiers borrowed from his Romantic masters a few of
the images he most frequently used. The comparison of Paris and a
furnace, developed in "Exil," was taken, as we have already
suggested, from the poem by Vigny entitled "Paris." An image as-
sociating life with the flow of water and man with a boat or sailor
upon the water, which Villiers used in "Barcarolle" and repeated in
"A mon ami Amédée Le Menant," "Lasciate ogni speranza," "Sur un
rocher" *(Préludes)*, and *Hermosa*, had been used not only by Lamartine in "Le Lac" but also by Hugo in "Oceano nox" (1840) and by
Musset in "Souvenir." Similarly, the image of death as an abyss
(abîme, gouffre), popularized by Lamartine ("Le Lac") and Hugo
("Tristesse d'Olympio"), was used by Villiers in "De profundis
clamavi," "Lasciate ogni speranza," and *Hermosa*.

Moreover, it is probable that Villiers borrowed rhythms chiefly
from Musset and Gautier.[31] Stanzas containing six lines of six syllables, which he used in "Prière indienne," had already been used by
Musset in "Le Lever" (1830) and Gautier in "Fantaisie IX" (1845).
Stanzas with six lines of twelve syllables (Alexandrines), used in
"Exil," are found not only in Gautier's "Le Coin du feu" (1832) but
also in Musset's "Namouna" (1832) and his poem "A la Malibran"
published in 1836 (from which, incidentally, Villiers took the
epigraph for his "De profundis clamavi"). Gautier wrote "Serment"

(1832) and Musset "Madame la marquise" (1830) and "A une fleur"
(1841) in stanzas of four octosyllabic verses; Villiers composed
"Zaïra" and "Découragement," using the same type of verse. A
stanza composed of three Alexandines followed by a line of six syllables, as in Villiers' "Lasciate ogni speranza," had already been used
by Musset in "Souvenir" (as well as by Lamartine in "Le Lac").
Gautier had already written six line stanzas with two Alexandrines
alternating with a line of six syllables ("Le Cavalier poursuivi"
[1832], "La Vie dans la mort" [1838]) as well as six line stanzas
containing two Alexandrines alternating with an octosyllabic line
("Le Bengali" [1832], "Pensée de minuit" [1838]); Villiers used the
twelve and six syllable combination in "A mon ami Amédée Le
Menant" and the twelve and eight combination in "Aurore." And in
"Les Souhaits" (1832), Gautier employed five line stanzas, containing an Alexandrine, followed by an octosyllabic line, then by two
Alexandrines and another octosyllabic line in succession; this is
exactly the arrangement Villiers used in "Primavera." All in all,
approximately half the rhythms Villiers used in his poetry had an-
tecedents in Musset's and Gautier's works.

Besides being partly derivative from the poetry of the Romantics,
it is indisputable that Villiers' poetry contains many weaknesses.
First of all, in his poems, Villiers used numerous hackneyed cir-
cumlocutions (periphrases), which, it must be admitted, his Romantic masters themselves did not always manage to avoid. For instance, he described the moon as the "silver star" in "Guitare" (OC,
X, 27) and as the "evening star" in "Sur un rocher" (139). He called
the ocean a "swelling flood" in "Exil" (22), and in "A mon ami
Amédée Le Menant" he described it as the "blue furrow" (133). In
Hermosa he used such periphrases as "liqueur of sleep" (59), "si-
dereal halo" (78), and "celestial crowns" (93), while in Chant du
Calvaire he called night a "flood of darkness" and the stars "golden
fires" (143).

In addition, Villiers' images (like those of his Romantic masters,
for that matter) were not always well chosen. The image of a
"forehead" which "bends in the evening winds like a lily on its stem"
("Exil" [OC, X, 21]) is risible because there is not enough visual
similarity between a forehead and body and a lily and stem. The
comparison of butterflies with Don Juan in the poem "Natura divina" (OC, X, 115) is also ill-chosen. Although Don Juan and butterflies are alike in that they both float from object to object, alight-
ing, pollinating, then moving on, butterflies do not possess qualities

like insensitivity, cruelty, and perhaps sinfulness that one ordinarily associates with the don. The simile Villiers used in "Lasciate ogni speranza"—"Mon esprit est semblable aux rochers, dont les cimes,/ Voyant s'enfuir les flots, penchent leurs antres nus / Sur leurs propres abîmes" (*OC*, X, 142)—is too overwrought and inconsistent with the direct expression of sadness and the uncomplicated syntax in the other verses of the poem.[32]

Furthermore, some of Villiers' poems are characterized by substantial rhetorical bombast, which admittedly at times also marked the poetry of the great Romantics. For example, a patriotic poem that Villiers wrote in response to British newspapers—"Une Façon d'imiter M. de Pompignan" (*Préludes*)—contains stanza after stanza of inflated and self-righteous language: "Englishmen, you have done despicable acts: / You have insulted, with most staining attacks, / A flag before which you have all trembled. / Behold, in truth, these things are cowardly" (*OC*, X, 111). Although many verses of the poem "De profundis clamavi" are touching, at least one stanza, containing a series of repetitious questions, borders on the rhetorical and bombastic:

> Puis, le réveil! la mort! l'existence qui change!
> O Temps! vieillard glacé! qu'as-tu fait de mon ange?
> Où l'as-tu mise, hélas! et froide, et pour toujours?
> Qu'as-tu fait de l'enfant jeune et pleine de charmes,
> Qu'as-tu fait du sourire et qu'as-tu fait des larmes,
>   Oh! qu'as-tu fait de nos amours? (*OC*, X, 131)[33]

And Villiers' language in *Hermosa* is on occasion rhetorical, as when Don Juan tries to explain to Hermosa the sad facts of death; his highly exclamatory language is ill-suited to his feelings of sorrow, regret, and tragedy:

> Paix du foyer natal! honneur, trésor fragile!
> Puissance, vacillant sur un trône d'argile!
> Prière, humble bonheur! gloire, sanglant plaisir!
> Toi, science, mot plein de vides insondables!
> Voilà les vanités de nos sorts misérables:
>   Notre seul but est de mourir! (*OC*, X, 69)[34]

Villiers' poetry contains three additional weaknesses. First, Villiers' rhymes (most of which are considered "weak"[35]), appear in some poems unnatural and contrived. In "Une Façon d'imiter M. de

Pompignan" (*OC*, X, 111), Villiers rhymes "trous" (the final *s* is silent) with "tous" (ordinarily the final *s* is pronounced when the adjective is alone). At other times, superfluous or lifeless words are added to the verse to complete a rhyme. For example, in "A Mme la comtesse de C . . . " (*OC*, X, 127) Villiers wrote: "I was very young then, and you too, I think"; and in *Hermosa* (*OC*, X, 86): "Don Juan answered: 'The twenty-seventh year / Cuts, between my brows, its natural line [*sa ride spontanée*].' " At still other times, as in "A mon ami Amédée Le Menant" and "Découragement," Villiers so contorts the word order to create a rhyme that the poetry becomes almost incomprehensible. The former poem reads: "Tu t'arrêtes, cherchant quelle route a suivie / Ta barque au sillon bleu" (*OC*, X, 133), and the latter is even worse: "Aux accents de l'hymne sacrée / Que chantait sous le grand ciel nu / Toute chose à peine créée / A son Créateur inconnu" (*OC*, X, 137).[36]

Second, with some of his longer lyric poems, notably "De profundis clamavi" (78 lines) and "A mon ami Amédée Le Menant" (66 lines), Villiers tried to develop too many ideas. In the former poem (*OC*, X, 129–32), for instance, he touched upon nature's indifference ("Nothing has changed in beautiful days"), the indifference of God ("Lord, you are mighty, but you are severe!"), the misery of the poet (" . . . it is finished on earth"), the cruelty of time ("O Time! icy old man! what have you done with my angel?"), nature's benevolence ("See how well the flowers near tombs grow! / One would say the young homeward doves sow / Bouquets to bid us sad farewell"), and the pleasure that suffering brings ("sorrow has its charms"). In the poem dedicated to Le Menant (*OC*, X, 133–36), he wrote about life's inscrutability (" 'Why did I grow up?' "), destiny ("In the mist of the seas, Destiny, gloomy beacon, / Raises a fiery finger"), man's cruelty ("Instead of helping one another, all men, these brothers / Hate one another"), love as salvation ("And, seeking in love a supreme refuge"), and man's essential solitude ("And every illusion, Hope, friendship, kindness, sublime trust, / Fall around him"). In reality, none of these themes is explored with any profundity, and as a result, the two lyrics seem rambling and without dramatic progression.

Finally, in Villiers' two long poems, *Hermosa* and *Chant du Calvaire*, temporal, thematic, and narrative unity is disrupted by numerous digressions and apostrophes to the reader. In *Hermosa*, the story of a young girl who meets Don Juan, falls in love with him, is left by him, and becomes a courtesan because "Only one [love] was no longer to fill this broken heart / Nor to be enough to fill the void of her soul" (*OC*, X, 102), parenthetic material plays such a prominent role and is developed to such length that the reader actually loses the thread of the plot. The author himself seems to be conscious of this danger, for at least once before resuming the narrative he warns of an imminent return and attempts to refresh the reader's memory:

> In short,—and our Hermosa?—This prelude is bizarre! . . .
> Hither, my cup of Cyprian wine, my cigar,
>   —Let us take up again our tale.

XVIII

> I had left you, I think, at the ball of count
> Antonio, by night, as mirthful swarms mount
> The palace steps . . .   (*OC*, X, 42–43)

Because of the preponderance of parenthetical material in *Hermosa*, it takes Villiers fifty stanzas to arrange the meeting of his heroine with Don Juan, the first crucial event in the poem. Although the disputations in *Chant du Calvaire* about the state of religion in the nineteenth century (*OC*, X, 148–52, 176–78) are less frequent than the digressions in *Hermosa*, they are no less abrupt and no less disruptive of the poem's narrative unity. They seriously mar an otherwise imaginative piece of writing.

B.   *Virtues of Villiers' Poetry*

Despite the weakness inherent in Villiers' poetry and in spite of its partly derivative nature, it still remains true that many of his poems are charming, imaginative, and inventive. In *Fantaisies nocturnes*, there are two works that merit attention. "Zaïra" (*OC*, X, 31–33), a poem about an Arab girl who declines a stranger's invitation to run away with him and chooses to remain faithful to her true love, is a good example of the way Villiers initially develops two simultaneous actions ("The setting sun was fading"; "The Arab was driving his coursers") and then unites them to form the basic conflict of the poem ("Before her [the young girl], the traveler haulted his untamed horse; / And bending suddenly, he said:"). At the same time, Villiers suggests the richness of the southern landscape by appealing not only to the reader's vision ("starlit dusk," "green leaves") but also to his tactile ("A warm air, like a breath,/ . . . Flowed lazily") and auditory senses ("The plane trees and the palms rustled [*froissaient*]").

In "Guitare" (*OC*, X, 27–28), perhaps the most successful of the poems contained in the *Fantaisies nocturnes*, Villiers evokes, through an appeal to the reader's vision ("Where sparkles . . . The silver star," "light leafy branches") and especially to his senses of touch ("The winds . . . blend") and of smell ("flowers," "orange trees"), the languid, romantic nights of Spain. The first stanza introduces the theme of love: Singing and dancing have ceased ("Spain. . . / No longer listens to mandolins"), women are drowsy ("Many beautiful eyes will close"), and the hour for courting is at hand ("It is time to love"). In the second stanza, the gypsy ceases playing ("Hangs his guitar on the plane tree"); the poet coaxes a girl to turn her attention again to love ("Let us love again"). In the final stanza, the poet urges the girl to yield to love at every opportunity ("Let us love forever"), for love, like the delicate orange blossoms, must soon wither and die ("They must wither, in autumn, / The orange trees and our love"). The languid and listless atmosphere that Villiers creates in these stanzas is reinforced by the poem's rhythm. Three eight syllable lines and one four syllable line must, in most cases, be read together without pause, assuring a slow and heavy cadence.

In *Les Préludes*, there are three poems that are written with much charm. Two of them, "Hier au soir" and "A son chevet," which incidentally remind one of Unamuno's *Incidentes domésticos* (1907) and which predate them by almost fifty years,[37] evoke simple, domestic incidents and the poet's reaction to them. In the former poem (*OC*, X, 117), the first two stanzas relate the incident: A woman reprimands the poet for spending too much time with books ("all those morose thinkers") and invites him to leave them and come into her "shade" where "one still finds flowers." The juxtaposition of flowers and shade is paradoxical but very significant. In traditional fashion, the flowers connote life and vitality, while the dark shade suggests calm, repose, and sexual experience. The final stanza of the poem relates the poet's reaction: He is moved by the woman's beauty and concern; full of happiness, he takes her hand and softly kisses it. The gratitude the poet feels for the woman's concern and the tenderness of his love are subtlely intimated by his smile, his trembling, and his soft kiss.

The first two stanzas of the poem "A son chevet" (*OC*, X, 121) also relate an incident. The poet looks in on his love asleep and admires her beauty ("How I love to look at my love who lies / Sleeping in her beauty!"). Following a description of her beauty ("graceful softness," "smiling," "Your mouth is of coral"), the second stanza ends on a disquieting note, for the night light casts an "uncertain glimmer" (*une lueur douteuse*) on the sleeper's face. To be sure, the mention of light realistically explains why the poet can distinguish at all his love's features; but, in addition, the words "lueur douteuse" set the reader on guard and prepare him for the sad news of the next stanza: the woman's health is faltering. The final stanza recounts the poet's reaction to the sight of his ailing love. Despite his desire to awaken her and be with her, he realizes that sleep is a respite from misery and wishes that she find joy in that sleep ("May her soul, having momentarily fled from here, / In ideal gardens gather everlasting flowers!").

A third poem in the collection, "Primavera" (*OC*, X, 119–20), is noteworthy for its structure as well as for its sensory appeal and its musicality. The poem is divided into four stanzas. In the first three stanzas, the poet describes the coming of spring. It arrives almost imperceptibly with the singing of birds and soft winds. Then its presence becomes more marked with the appearance of rays of sunlight, flowers, grazing animals, green plains, violets and butterflies, and finally a golden sun against blue skies. The last two lines of the third stanza ("It's all a prayer in which heav'n invites us / To feel young once again") form a transition to the fourth stanza, in which the poet asks his love to learn something from nature: The sunray conducts man's vision toward God, the renaissance of nature encourages man to hope, and the violet ever courted by the butterfly tells him to yield to love.

Villiers evokes a vivid picture of nature by appealing not only to one's vision ("the green plain," "the white butterflies," "the blue [sky]," "the golden sun") and hearing ("Already the gentle birds are singing," "the lowing [*mugissants*] herds") but also to one's tactile ("The warm winds blow [*soufflent*]") and olfactory senses ("the violets' breath," "heavy with fragrances"). In the second stanza he intentionally confuses two senses—a technique called synesthesia for which Baudelaire and the Symbolists were to be famous—by describing the effect the colors of spring create in terms of a concert. Villiers' use of alliteration (the repetition of the letter f in the first stanza), his use of onomatopoeic sounds (the letters v, f, and s to characterize the winds; the word "mugissants" to describe the herds), as well as his alternation of long (Alexandrine) and short (octosyllabic) lines all contribute to the musicality of the poem.

The *Chant du Calvaire*, certainly the most imaginative work in the *Premières Poésies*, is rightly viewed as a triptych; each of its three cantos, which bear foreign titles and Latin epigraphs purportedly drawn from the Psalms,[38] evokes a moment in the day of Christ's crucifixion. The first canto describes Christ's actual death, the second, a pagan orgy supposedly taking place near Calvary, and the third, Mary Magdalene's supposed vigil at the foot of the cross. Throughout the poem, Villiers contrasts the Christian love (*agape*, *caritas*) exemplified by Christ and Magdalene with the sensual love (*eros*) of pagans.

Canto I (*OC*, X, 145–52) is divided into three sections. The first section paints a contrast between a pagan celebration in honor of Venus, goddess of love (ll. 1–19, 22–35, 39–44), and Christ's sacrifice on the cross nearby (ll. 20–21, 36–38, 45–49). This section ends with Christ's death and his mournful cry: "Héli! Lamma Sabactanni!" ("My God, why hast thou forsaken me?"), which serves as title of the canto. Section two describes the strange occurrences that follow Christ's death. The opening of tombs (l. 8) is indeed recounted in the Bible (Matthew 27:52–53), but phenomena such as lightning (l. 9) and the opening sky (ll. 22–35) are apocryphal and added for dramatic effect. Moreover, contrary to biblical accounts in which darkness pervades the land from the sixth to ninth hour (Matthew 27:45–46; Mark 15:33–34; Luke 23:44–46), Villiers dramatically introduces the darkness at the ninth hour, the precise moment Christ expires (l. 1). It seems unfortunate to us that Villiers concludes the canto with a discussion of faith in the nineteenth century (section three), as it destroys continuity between Cantos I and II.

Canto II (*OC*, X, 153–72), esthetically the most complex of the poem, is divided into seven sections. After two introductory sections, in which Villiers returns to the contrast between a self-sacrificing Christ (sec. 1, l. 2; sec. 2, l. 22) and bacchanalian pagans (sec. 1, ll. 1, 3–10; sec. 2, ll. 1–21, 23–26), the poem, which has been up to this point narrative, assumes a dramatic form. The song of the slaves, a hymn of praise and devotion to Venus (section three), introduces four scenes (sections four to six), which constitute the center of Canto II and which expose the insensitivity of pagan love. Lyncéus, a "child of fifteen years," falls madly in love with the courtesan Sempronia, who offers herself to him with the words: "Oh! Be my universe, I shall be your night!" (scene 1). Moments later, amid a bacchanalian orgy and cries of "Evohë Bacchus" ("Hail, Bacchus"), whence the title of the canto, Sempronia offers herself to Sextus Lucius Marcellus (scene 3), who only moments before has been pining for the missing and delectable Magdalene (scene 2). Heartbroken by Sempronia's infidelity, Lyncéus throws himself into a river, while a nightingale, the bird of love, heartlessly begins its song again, and Sempronia intones the slaves' hymn to Venus (scene 4), which had introduced the dramatic part of the poem. As the hymn at the end of the drama parallels the hymn at the beginning, section seven, which is again narrative in form, parallels the two initial narrative sections. This final section serves as a transition to Canto III since it raises the question of Magdalene ("Where then was Magdalene?"), who is the subject of the last canto and for whom it is named.

Canto III (*OC*, X, 173–81), which returns to the site of the Crucifixion, is divided like Canto II into seven sections. The first three sections, unlike the biblical accounts (Matthew 27–28; Mark 15–16; Luke 23–24; John 19–20), describe Mary Magdalene, the former prostitute for whom Sextus Lucius Marcellus was pining, praying all alone at the feet of the dead but now resplendent Christ ("The crown of thorns, Like rays, / . . . Gleamed"), while pagan spirits tempt her to return to her old life. The last sections contrast the *caritas* and faith of Christ, which triumphed in the face of an ignominious death (section four), and that of Magdalene, which overcame the attraction of wealth and *eros* (section six), with the faithlessness, paganism, and desperation of modern man (sections five and seven). In the last line, Villiers expresses the wish that his century be mindful of Christ's suffering ("Like a last torch let us keep at least the Cross!").

Villiers' *Premières Poésies* are significant for several reasons. Although many poems in the collection lack originality and are marred most noticeably by bombast, superfluous lines, and contrived rhymes, some of the works are in truth artistically imaginative, well-executed, and worth reading. With the exception of the *Chant du Calvaire*, Villiers' most successful poems are short, delicate expressions of love between man and woman ("Chanson arabe," "Guitare," "Heir au soir," "A son chevet," "Primavera"). Moreover, as these poems testify, Villiers is most successful as a poet when he composes works that are not strictly lyric but basically narrative in form.

Besides its artistic value, this collection of poetry is important because it reveals something of Villiers' past and portends something of his future. It would be dangerous to reconstruct the poet's early life by relying heavily on his writings, since some poems only imitate themes and feelings popularized by the Romantics, while others probably contain details that have been "transmuted through projection and artistic distance."[39] Notwithstanding, the *Premières Poésies* do reveal Villiers as a sensitive young man, concerned with religious and philosophic matters, and very likely, the unhappy romances discussed in "De profundis clamavi" and "Lasciate ogni speranza" have some foundation in reality. In addition, the *Premières Poésies* foreshadow aspects of Villiers' subsequent writings. Not only does the collection contain themes, such as religion, the dangers of materialism, and the search for the ideal, to which Villiers will return, but the *Chant du Calvaire*, with its dramatic interlude, foreshadows his later interest in the theater, while most of his poems reveal a talent for narration, which will be fully exploited only with his short stories.

CHAPTER 2

The Years of Apprenticeship

I New Directions, Trips to Germany, Foreign and Civil War (1860–1871)

IN the two years after his move to Paris (1860–1862), Villiers not only strengthened ties with Baudelaire and Pontavice; collaborated on a magazine, *La Revue fantaisiste;* and became friendly with its editor, Catulle Mendès; but he also worked on a philosophical, occultist novel entitled *Isis.* The first part of the work appeared in August 1862. Despite some praise for this volume—Théodore de Banville perceived in it "the undeniable claw of genius"[1]—Villiers never finished the novel. It is possible that the scant attention most critics paid the first part or the loss of a second volume totally discouraged Villiers from completing it. Then too, it is possible that he himself tired of it, thinking his talents better suited to other forms of prose.[2] In any event, after the publication of the first part of *Isis,* Villiers turned to writing drama, in which he had shown an interest as early as 1855. Only in the late 1870s did Villiers return to novel writing, and then to begin *L'Eve future,* not to finish *Isis.*

One can well imagine that in these two years, despite devotion to his work, Villiers stayed out too late and caroused too much. Indeed, alarmed by the effect Paris life and the company of one Louise Dyonnet were having on his spiritual well-being, Villiers' family sought to wrest the young man from danger by sending him on a seven day retreat (13–20 September 1862) to the Benedictine monastery of Solesmes, west of Paris. This retreat failed to reform Villiers' life in the substantial way his parents hoped, and in less than a year's time (August 1863), Mlle de Kérinou informed Dom Guéranger, abbot of Solesmes, that Villiers' "cure was temporary" and that he "had [again] become attached to [that] horrible crea-

ture" (*Corr*, I, 58). As a result, Villiers was sent back to the monastery, where this time he met the Catholic apologist Louis Veuillot
(*Corr*, I, 62; *OC*, VI, 217–27). After ten days of retreat, however, he
fled with the help of his devoted friend Jean Marras, who sent him
the necessary funds (*Corr*, I, 60–63).

In the meantime, on the other side of Europe, the Greek people
had deposed their monarch, King Otho. Hoping to maintain stabil-
ity in a troubled area, the three protecting powers of Greece—
France, England, and Russia—set about to find a suitable candidate
for the vacant throne (1863). It was rumored in Paris that Napoleon
III's choice for king was none other than Count Jean-Marie Mathias
Philippe Auguste de Villiers de l'Isle-Adam, and Villiers himself
claimed that he was summoned to Napoleon's residence and questioned by the grand chamberlain of the palace. It is uncertain
whether these stories of Villiers' candidacy had any foundation in
reality, first because Villiers delighted in creating, encouraging, and
disseminating legends about himself, and second because, as Robert
du Pontavice implies, these rumors may well have been part of a
hoax engineered by a disgruntled actor endeavoring to pay Villiers
back for a trick he had once played on him.[3] Be that as it may,
nothing came of Villiers' supposed candidacy, and a Danish prince
was crowned king of Greece on 30 October 1863. Nevertheless,
Villiers was momentarily the focal point of Parisian gossip.

Of greater significance in Villiers' life were two events of 1864.
First, Villiers met Stéphane Mallarmé, then an English teacher at
the *collège* of Tournon and later to be hailed as the head of the
French Symbolist movement, probably at the home of Catulle
Mendès' father in Choisy-le-Roi, south of Paris. The two were destined to become lifelong friends. In the twenty-odd years of association, Mallarmé's philosophic and esthetic thought would be greatly
influenced by Villiers, whereas, in his tormented life, Villiers would
frequently be consoled by the poet's friendly and understanding
aid.[4] Second, to the utter jubilation, one can well imagine, of Mlle
de Kérinou and his parents, Villiers broke off in 1864 with Louise
Dyonnet. What was Villiers' reason? He claimed in a letter to Louise
that he simply no longer loved her (*Corr*, I, 70). But, in all likelihood, he ended the affair because the woman's infidelity—"It is
not," he wrote, "through lack of trust in me that you have sinned so
far" (*Corr*, I, 74)—was causing him an intolerable amount of suffering. In a poignant and candid moment, Villiers confessed: "I adored
you, Louise, and for a long time in the midst of overwhelming

sufferings; but you are right: every deep affection must be sacrificed for a comfortable night's rest. You made me dream a wretched dream" (*Corr*, I, 73). The affair, which caused Villiers so much pain, may have left its mark on his play *Elën* (1865) and the prose poem "A celle qui est morose" (1867), and Louise probably served as model for Clio la Cendrée and Annah Jackson, the cruel female protagonists in his later story "Le Convive des dernières fêtes" (*CC*, 97–127).[5]

Between excitement over his supposed candidacy for the Greek throne and anguish over Mme Dyonnet, Villiers did manage to devote some time to writing. He probably reread and revised in 1863–1864 the three act prose play he had begun in 1862, at the time of his first stay at Solesmes (*Corr*, I, 52, 55).[6] This was the aforementioned *Elën*, which was printed for private circulation on 14 January 1865. Then, in all likelihood, Villiers devoted most of 1865 to revising the five act play *Morgane*, a primitive version of which Villiers had purportedly sketched in 1855 (*Corr*, I, 31). Twenty-five copies of the revised version were finally printed in March 1866 by Guyon Francisque of Saint-Brieuc. Unfortunately, neither *Elën* nor *Morgane* fared very well. The first went completely unnoticed by the press. And, despite Mallarmé's praise (*Corr*, I, 109) and Villiers' initial hope for a theatrical engagement—"I have just completed five acts, a drama *Morgane*, it is accepted at the Gaîté," the author wrote to Joséphin Soulary on 1 September 1866 (*Corr*, I, 97)—the second play likewise neither gained the wide acclaim of critics nor was ever performed during Villiers' lifetime.

After the refusal of the latter play by theaters, Villiers seems to have experienced a sense of weariness and defeat.[7] Villiers' mental state is certainly understandable. The ten years during which he had hoped to establish his reputation as a writer (*Corr*, I, 30) had passed. In spite of his relentless hard work, including collaboration on the *Revue fantaisiste* (1861) and the *Parnasse contemporain* (1866), and despite the praise of everyone who knew him, Mallarmé and Henri de Régnier included,[8] Villiers had not in that time impressed the frivolous public and had not created one lasting literary monument. Not only had his poetry been forgotten and his novel abandoned, but now even his plays had been overlooked or rejected outright. No wonder Villiers' contempt for society was on the rise!

Yet, Villiers gave up neither writing nor his interest in the theater. Rather, he turned his attention momentarily to different literary genres. First, he tried his hand at prose poetry. It is thought that at

this time he wrote a whole series of prose poems in imitation of
Baudelaire and that most of them have been lost.[9] Two prose
poems, "El Desdichado" and the aforementioned "A celle qui est
morose," however, are definitely from this period and still extant,
having been published in the magazine *La Lune*.[10] Then, around
1866, Villiers turned to the short story, probably because of growing
fascination with the American short story writer Edgar Allan Poe.
Curiously, Baudelaire may have introduced Villiers to Poe's writings in French translation as early as 1862, but it was only now that
they seem to have had any effect upon him.[11] Villiers' first story,
"Claire Lenoir," appeared in the 13 October–1 December 1867
installments of the *Revue des Lettres et des Arts*, a weekly that he
himself had founded primarily to promote his own writings and that
he edited during its brief existence (13 October 1867–23 March
1868). This satiric tale revealed not only Villiers' debt to Poe but also
his continued interest in Hegel and occultism, as well as his recent
knowledge of a two volume work by the cabalist Eliphas Lévi entitled *Dogme et rituel de la haute magie*. A second short story by
Villiers also dealt with the occult. It was called "L'Intersigne" and
was likewise published serially in the pages of the *Revue des Lettres
et des Arts* (8 December 1867–12 January 1868). A third story,
"Azraël," was published on 26 June 1869 in Emile de Girardin's *La
Liberté*—the *Revue des Lettres* was now defunct—probably through
the intercession of Catulle Mendès, who collaborated frequently on
de Girardin's journal.

    Not only was Villiers' writing career beginning to look brighter,
but in the years following the disastrous affair with Louise Dyonnet,
Villiers fared much better in his choice of female companionship. In
fact, he seems to have become allied with women who offered him
great intellectual and emotional sustenance. In 1866, for instance, at
her father's home in Versailles, Villiers met Augusta Holmès, a
young, talented musician who would become a true friend (*OC*, XI,
106–13). In 1866–1867, he courted Estelle Gautier, the younger
daughter of the poet Théophile Gautier. Unfortunately, Villiers was
forced to give up wedding plans when his proud aristocratic family,
anxious that he marry a rich, and preferably noble, woman, objected
to the commoner with no great assets (*Corr*, I, 103). Then, in 1868,
along with Mallarmé, Catulle Mendès, and the poets Paul Verlaine,
Charles Cros, and François Coppée, Villiers became a frequent
guest at the Parisian soirées of Nina de Villard, "a lively and charming person" who "loved music and poetry and poets even more."[12]

It is probable that Villiers became her lover for a short while.[13] In any event, Mme de Villard and her gatherings made a strong impression on the writer, for years later he left an account of them entitled "Une Soirée chez Nina de Villard" (*OC*, XI, 81–86).

In the summer of 1869, Richard Wagner's opera *Das Rheingold* was to have its world premiere in Munich. Villiers, who had probably been introduced to Wagner's music by Baudelaire about 1860 and had become by 1867 one of the few ardent French admirers of the German composer (even able to play his works on the piano),[14] longed to attend the performance but did not have the resources. Rather craftily, he and two other fervent Wagnerites, Catulle Mendès and his wife Judith, elder daughter of Théophile Gautier, persuaded several French journals to pay their way to Munich, theoretically to report on the International Exposition of Painting, to be inaugurated on 1 August in the Bavarian capital. Judith, who had corresponded with Wagner, arranged for the trio to stop at the composer's home in Triebschen near Lucerne en route to Germany. The travelers arrived at Wagner's in the middle of July and spent nine days with him listening to his music. Then they proceeded to Munich, where they stayed until 13 September, gathering information on the exposition and attending rehearsals of *Das Rheingold* (the opera's premiere being postponed to 22 September). They spent five additional days at Triebschen on their way home. Villiers was overpowered by the presence of Wagner and by his music. His descriptions of the composer read like a litany: "Wagner, he is indeed the man we had dreamt of; he is the genius such as appears once in a thousand years . . ." (*Corr*, I, 134). In fact, he was so overawed by the experience that he failed to submit promptly his article on the exposition. When he did complete the article, he had to confess to his readers: "It is too late to speak to you about the Exposition . . . that already old piece of news."[15] He proceeded to talk, not about the exhibit, but about the delights of Munich.

Upon returning to Paris, Villiers revised a play, *La Révolte*, which he had sketched in 1869 (*Corr*, I, 148), carried with him to Germany, and read to Wagner on the last night of his visit.[16] Despite his success with the short story, it seems that Villiers still desired, above all, to gain critical acclaim as a playwright. Moreover, encouraged by the success of Wagner's musical dramas in Germany, he hoped to initiate theatrical reform in France with this play (*OC*, VII, xx). The one act play in prose was performed, thanks to the intervention of Alexandre Dumas *fils*, at the Vaudeville Theater on 6

May 1870. Unfortunately, it was little understood and turned out to be a miserable failure.

Because of this disappointment, Villiers must have accepted all the more willingly an offer by various Parisian newspapers to send him, along with Catulle and Judith Mendès, to Germany to report on two events scheduled for June, a Wagner festival in Weimar and the premiere of Wagner's *Die Walküre* in Munich. Departing on 10 June, the trio went first to Weimar, where they saw performances of *Der Fliegende Holländer, Tannhäuser, Lohengrin*, and *Die Meistersinger*, and where in Franz Liszt's home Villiers purportedly read "Claire Lenoir" to the utter delight of the grand duke of Saxe-Weimar (*Corr*, I, 155; *OC*, V, 195–209). Then they journeyed southward to Munich, where they attended performances of *Das Rheingold* and Die *Walküre* (not the premiere, however, since they arrived too late), and where on 19 July 1870 they were surprised by the declaration of war between France and Prussia. Momentarily, Villiers served as war correspondent. He wrote, for instance, an article entitled "Les Premiers Jours de la Guerre de 1870," published by *Le Constitutionnel*, in which he described for his French readers the situation in Munich and his impressions of the Prussian army stationed there.[17] The three foreigners, however, judged it imprudent to remain too long in enemy territory. En route to France, they traveled to Triebschen to pay homage to Wagner. This time, because of the war, relations between the German host and his French guests "remained delicate during the entire stay."[18]

Upon leaving Triebschen and before returning to Paris, Judith, Catulle, and Villiers stopped in Avignon to visit Mallarmé, who was then on the faculty of the local *lycée*. Villiers, in fact, returned home only a few days before the defeat of the French by the Prussians at Sedan, Napoleon III's fall from power, and the proclamation of the Third Republic on 4 September 1870. When the Prussians, instead of retiring or offering lenient peace terms to the new republic, besieged the capital in an attempt to bring the defeated nation to its knees (23 September), Count Villiers, the loyal son of France, responded by taking command of a division of the national guard of Paris. All was in vain. After four months of seige, the weary city capitulated to the enemy on 28 January 1871.

Peace, however, did not last very long. On 18 March, republican Paris rebelled against the conservative provisional French government sitting in Versailles and established its own independent government (Commune). Villiers' loyalties, like those of many Parisians, were torn. At first, he favored the cause of the Communards, even contributing to one of their newspapers, *Le Tribun du peuple*. Later, he was relieved when government forces finally crushed the insurrection after nine weeks of bloody fighting (18 March–27 May).[19] As if the tribulation of civil war were not enough, 13 August 1871 brought Villiers an additional sorrow, the death of his great-aunt Mlle de Kérinou. The intensity of Villiers' grief can be felt by reading the letters he wrote to his old friends Amédée Le Menant des Chesnais (*Corr*, I, 171) and Dom Guéranger of Solesmes (*Corr*, I, 172), asking their prayers for the repose of her soul.

The period from Villiers' settling in Paris to the Commune and Mlle de Kérinou's death (1860–1871) can justly be considered his term of apprenticeship. In these years, Villiers experienced virtually all the influences—Baudelaire, Poe, Hegel, Mallarmé, Wagner, and occultism—that would in some way mark his future artistic production. Moreover, in this eleven year period, he tried his hand at all the literary genres—novel, drama, prose poem, short story—to which he would subsequently return and which he would later handle with more mastery. Indeed, his experimentation with the short story in imitation of Poe revealed a special affinity for this form. Half of his works would turn out to be short prose, and through this medium he would eventually gain a reputation. Finally, probably through Poe and Baudelaire's influence, Villiers experimented (in "Claire Lenoir," for example) with irony and satiric humor, and these were to become trademarks of his later writings. As a result of contact with other writers and literary experimentation in 1860–1871, Villiers was becoming aware of his own particular talents as a writer. The insights gained in these years would enable him to write his masterpieces of the 1770s and 1880s.

II Isis

Villiers' first novel, *Isis* (1862), set in Italy at the end of the eighteenth century, traces the destiny of two extraordinary characters, the Florentine marquise, Tullia Fabriana, and the German count, Wilhelm de Strally-d'Anthas. Having fled the "banal commerce of the world" (*OC*, IX, 57) and attained a complete mastery of knowledge under the aegis of the Egyptian goddess, Isis, "face of Creation" (115), Tullia chooses to share the mysteries of the Ideal and its power with the count and make him a propagator of it. The novel breaks off after the enchantress takes possession of Wilhelm's mind in a prophetic vision and the two beings fuse into one. In the

remainder of the novel, Tullia would probably have fallen in love
with the count, and Villiers would have demonstrated the incompatibility of worldly desires and human emotions with devotion to
the Ideal. This ending seems likely not simply because he would
later develop that theme in *Elën, Morgane,* and *Axël,* [20] but chiefly
because he had already showed himself as thinking along similar
lines in the case of Mary Magdalene, heroine of *Chant du Calvaire,*
and because Wilhelm's prophetic dream at the conclusion of volume
I clearly suggests this.

Although it is doubtful whether Villiers read Hegel's works—his
knowledge of the philosopher was probably restricted to what he
learned from Pontavice de Heussey (to whom *Isis* is dedicated) and
gleaned from Auguste Véra's *Introduction à la philosophie de Hegel*
(1855)[21]—or really understood the essence of Hegelian thought,[22]
Isis clearly reflects currents of this idealistic philosophy. In fact, the
novel may have been undertaken to illustrate that philosophy.[23]
Three ideas fundamental to Hegel's system—the division of the
world into positive reality and absolute ideal, the supremacy of
spirit over matter, and the evolution of humanity toward a state of
perfect awareness—are at the heart of Tullia Fabriana's beliefs. Furthermore, other concepts of Hegel, which have little to do with the
novel's plot and are admittedly "decorative,"[24] are alluded to in
philosophical digressions (*OC,* IX, 100–101, 116–17). By no means
exclusively Hegelian in inspiration, the novel is also the first of
Villiers' works to bear a strong element of occultism; Villiers may
have inherited these theories from Pontavice, Jean Marras, Bulwer-
Lytton's *Zanoni* (translated 1843, 1858), or numerous popular man-
uals.[25] The final chapters of *Isis,* for example, touch on such occult
subjects as metempsychosis, union of souls, prophetic nature of
dreams, and mystical powers of the enchantress.

In all fairness, there are some noteworthy elements in this novel.
Besides the occult themes of metempsychosis and the aloof enchantress (which, incidentally, will be picked up by the Symbolists,
notably Mallarmé[26]), Villiers develops other themes, already enunciated in the *Premières Poésies,* that call into question the
nineteenth century's fundamental faith in science and progress. Not
only does he condemn the spiritual deprivation of his age, but he
also points out the fatuousness of scientific progress that neglects
human values ("Progress has become a doubtful concept and necessity . . . . Like the gods and kings, Art, Inspiration and Love flee"
[*OC,* IX, 92]). Another noteworthy element in the novel is Villiers'

masterful evocation, through his sensitivity to visual detail and the musicality of his prose, of the palaces, colorful fêtes, and intrigue of eighteenth century Florence, as well as the mysterious aura that enshrouds Tullia's life. Finally, Villiers' use of metaphoric language in the prophetic vision at the novel's end (227–31) commands attention. In the vision, Wilhelm imagines that Tullia is swimming in the "crystalline waters" of a "deep pool" bathed by "moonlight" filtering through the "cypresses;" that the seductive "siren" is joined first by swans, "attracted by her whiteness," and then by Wilhelm himself; and that, after leaving the water, the two nude protagonists, "two garden statues [taking] advantage of the darkness to come back to life," exchange kisses in the "perfumed air" amid "thick clusters" of flowers. The cypress trees mentioned at the beginning of the dream evoke death, Tullia's death to the senses, while the act of swimming in clear, deep waters bathed in light implies a purified, contemplative existence. Whiteness and swans, associated with Tullia, reinforce this idea of purity. In the final segment of the dream, Villiers suggest the couple's rediscovery of sensuality and emotion; like statues come to life, they leave the clear water and enter a dark garden, teeming with life.

Despite these positive qualities, it must be admitted that the completed parts of this work reveal serious deficiencies. First, as Huysmans intimates in his novel *A Rebours*, *Isis* contains every Romantic cliché, from secret dungeons and daggers to rope ladders and mysterious doors, that Villiers could recall from his reading of old melodramas.[27] More significantly, narration in the novel is constantly interrupted by digression. It is true that some of these digressions, such as the ones on Tullia's early life (51–63) and her appearance (65–71), may be justified, for they do provide vital information about the principal character. Nevertheless, many of the digressions, notably the ones on modern times (91–98, 220–22), Hegelian philosophy (100–101, 116–17), the Fabriana family history (74–78), and Tullia's library (83–86), have such a tenuous connection with the plot and are at times so clumsily introduced (51, 65, 220) that they destroy the novel's unity and tax the reader's patience. Finally, the novel is virtually static. Because of the preponderance of digressions, it takes Villiers one hundred and thirty pages to introduce Wilhelm to Tullia and an additional sixty-odd pages to initiate any real action in the story. Ironically, once the characters have come together and the story has the possibility of developing, the work breaks off and is never resumed. In short, then, with this novel, Villiers had difficulty avoiding clichés, developing and sustaining action, and coordinating component parts into a unified whole. It can be said that the same defects evident in the earlier *Hermosa* and, to a lesser degree, in the *Chant du calvaire* also mar *Isis*.

III   *Early Dramas*

A. Elën

The first act of Villiers' *Elën* (1865) takes place outside the Dresden Arms Inn "at an indefinite time" (*OC*, VIII, 198). Motivated by jealousy, rage, and desperation, Mme de Walhburg has hired Tannucio to kill Andréas de Rosenthal, who does not reciprocate her love, as well as his mistress, Countess Elën, whom Andréas adores. After Rosenthal confesses that he is seeking exile in Iceland because of unrequited love for Elën and that no other woman can touch him ("I am of those who can love but once" [219]), Mme de Walhburg drops the flowers from her waist, giving Tannucio the signal that he is to delay no longer in executing their plans. Samuel Wissler, a young, idealistic student just home from abroad, picks up the flowers and returns them to Mme de Walhburg, who exits saying: "Keep them, sir, and may they bring you happiness" (221). After denouncing impure love ("I wish to keep my soul's purity" [224]) and declining an invitation to dine with his friend Goetz and a group of carefree students, appropriately singing "Fratres gaudeamus," Samuel falls asleep on a moss bed near the inn. Elën passes by, espies Samuel, and takes him home to "love three days" without revealing her name and then "leave him alone with [her] memory" (232).

Act II, set in the countess's palace, opens with Tannucio's reciting "Guitare," a poem that was originally published in the *Premières Poésies* (*OC*, X, 27–28) and which, with its emphasis on sensual love, fittingly ushers us into the private retreat of Elën. Following a visit from Mme de Walhburg, who futilely attempts "to conciliate without a murder" (*OC*, VIII, 239) by asking the countess either to cure Andréas of his love or to leave the city, Elën orders that Samuel, of whom she has tired ("I no longer love this young man . . . ; I've realized my dream" [253–54]), be drugged and taken from the palace. From his drugged body, she demands the flowers that, unbeknownst to her, the student received from Mme de Walhburg.

Tannucio presents them to her, having first poured on them a deadly poison. Elën dies amid a costume ball, attended by Andréas, who retrieves the poisoned flowers.

Act III, like Act I, takes place outside the Dresden Arms Inn. Samuel is awakening from a prophetic nightmare in which he not only sees Elën and himself in a "compartment of Hell" (268) but also hears Elën boasting triumphantly that he has been "darkened by her love" (271). He discounts, nevertheless, any significance to this dream and enthusiastically announces to Goetz that he has just met a woman, holy and pure, in whom all his ideals are found. Samuel's paean is interrupted by the Latin hymn "Dies Irae" and a funeral procession bearing a courtesan who, Goetz explains, died at a ball celebrating her breakup with a boring lover. When Samuel recognizes the dead Elën, he realizes that he has been deceived, has sacrificed his ideals on an unworthy being, and is now only a "phantom of what [he] was" (280). He departs on a pilgrimage. Presenting Mme de Walhburg with the flowers taken from Elën's body (283), Andréas takes leave of the woman, forgiving her for what she has done. Only Tannucio, who picks up Samuel's discarded purse, is left happy.

It is clear that *Elën* consists of two distinct intrigues. The first, involving Elën and Samuel, is by far the more compelling. One can share the sufferings of a young man whose illusions are shattered. One can also understand a woman whose fears of intimacy propel her into countless affairs and prevent her from truly loving anybody. The second, involving Mme de Walhburg, Andréas, and Elën, however, lacks the "depth and [human] truth" of the first.[28] For one thing, it is hard to imagine that unrequited love could drive Mme de Walhburg to the melodramatic measures it does. For another, it is not entirely clear why Mme de Walhburg, who seems so determined in Act I to have both Andréas and Elën killed, should change her mind in Act II and have Tannucio inflict revenge solely on Elën.

While distinct, these two intrigues converge at three points in the play: in Act I, when Samuel returns the flowers to Mme de Walhburg; in Act II, with Mme de Walhburg's visit to Elën; and in Act III, when Samuel recognizes the dead countess. Unfortunately, at least two of these meetings seem uncalled for by the circumstances of the play. It seems contrived, for instance, that Samuel should arrive from abroad at the precise moment that Mme de Walhburg dramatically loosens the flowers from her waist. Similarly, it is too coincidental that Samuel happens to awake from his drugged sleep and be watching at the exact moment the cortege passes.

Notwithstanding the coincidences, the implausibility of Mme de Walhburg's character, and the general cloak-and-dagger nature of the play, there are three aspects of *Elën* worth noting. The first is, as we have suggested, the intrigue between Elën and Samuel. This intrigue has a ring of truth that is lacking in the other parts of the drama. Indeed, the genuineness of the emotions expressed by Samuel has led some critics to suggest that the dramatic episode— although probably influenced by Musset's *On ne badine pas avec l'amour* (1834), Wagner's *Tannhäuser* (1845), and Gautier's "La Morte amoureuse" (1845), whence the epigraph to the second edition—owes much to Villiers' own experience (conceivably with Mme Dyonnet, since the play was not published until 1865).[29] Second, for the first time in any of his works, Villiers uses irony (probably stemming from association with Baudelaire[30]). For example, the flowers bestowed on Samuel in the hopes that they will bring him happiness actually prove to be a source of unhappiness for him since they not only cause the countess's death but also set in motion events that will lead to his awareness of Elën's deception. Likewise, in order to avoid contamination of his ideals, Samuel refuses to dine with the hedonistic students; yet this refusal permits his meeting Elën, who will succeed where the students could not. It is ironic, above all, that Samuel believes Elën to be a paragon of holiness. Finally, possibly inspired by Wagner, Villiers effectively employs musical motifs—the traditional student song "Fratres gaudeamus," the hymn "Dies Irae," and his own poem accompanied by guitar— either to intimate character traits, as in the case of the students, or to create an atmosphere, as with the hymn and his own poem.

B. Morgane

Action in Villiers' *Morgane* (1866) is more complex than in *Elën*. There are more characters in Villiers' second drama, and what is more, actions are motivated not only by love or lack of it but also by political ambition. Unlike *Elën*, *Morgane* paints a conflict between love and political desire.

The drama, possibly suggested by Théophile Gautier's novel *Souvenirs d'une favorite*,[31] is set in the Italy of the 1790s, where King Ferdinand and Queen Marie-Caroline have handed virtual control of the Two Sicilies to the English ambassadrice, Lady

Hamilton. Morgane, duchess of Poleastro, is plotting against them and seeks a man to replace Ferdinand. In the fortress of Città-Lazzara in Calabra, Morgane meets Sergius d'Albamah, a political prisoner of the king. Without knowing that Sergius has a legitimate claim to the Sicilian throne, Morgane decides on him as Ferdinand's successor. After killing Marquis d'Ast, emissary of Lady Hamilton, the two successfully evade the royal guards.

In Act II, set in her castle in Calabra, Morgane persuades her goddaughter Sione, who wants to enter a convent because of an unhappy romance, to test her religious vocation by accompanying her to Naples. She then joins an idealistic Sergius and the other conspirators, who plan to overthrow Ferdinand by inciting a popular uprising through the elimination of food supplies. Although Sergius, who has fallen in love with Morgane, is reluctant to carry out the plan ("There is not enough room in my heart for human ambition" [*OC*, VIII, 65]), Morgane, no less in love with Sergius, is driven by dreams of power ("Your love has tripled my thirst and my strength: I have a passion for the throne" [64]). Sione enters and recognizes Sergius as the man she once loved and still does; Sergius recognizes the girl he could have loved (88).

Act III takes place in Naples at the court of the Kingdom of the Two Sicilies; revolution has broken out. Morgane is playing chess with her rival, Lady Hamilton. Suspecting that Morgane has engineered Sergius' prison escape and is responsible for the death of her emissary, Hamilton almost arrests Morgane, but a page deceitfully convinces Hamilton that D'Ast is well. After Hamilton, disguised as a magician, proclaims in the midst of a ball that Sergius is one of those men whose "best constructed plans collapse" (111), the announcement is made that D'Ast has indeed been killed. It is now too late for Hamilton to take action, for Sergius enters and challenges the king. Hamilton reminds Sergius that a guest has no right to challenge his host. The conspirators retire and surround the palace.

In Act IV, near Morgane's camp, the witch Monna Jahëli predicts to Sergius that he will die from a falling statue and that Morgane will fall victim to a glove she will never put on. Meanwhile, heralded by the anthem "God save the Queen," Lady Hamilton arrives, ostensibly to acknowledge Morgane's victory, to renounce any loyalties to Ferdinand, and to swear allegiance to her rival. In a manner befitting Shakespeare's Iago. she craftily claims that Sergius is using Morgane to "regain his throne and offer it to his mistress [Sione]"

(160). Morgane believes these lies, especially when by chance she sees Sione taking leave of Sergius. In an attempt to avenge herself on Sergius and Sione, the angry Morgane sabotages the uprising by ordering the soldiers surrounding the palace to retire. Her mission accomplished, Hamilton prepares Morgane for death. Following the death of Morgane's page Leone, Sergius appears from nowhere and disrupts the duchess's execution.

Act V opens with Morgane, awaiting execution in a Salerno convent. A nun comes to prepare her for death; it is Sione. After the latter convinces Morgane that she has been cruelly deceived by Hamilton, Sergius arrives to take his beloved away. "All is not lost," he says, "we still have love" (186–87). It is, however, too late. While the voice of Monna Jahëli resounds in the background, Morgane falls victim to Hamilton's poisoned glove and dies, begging Sergius to join her in eternity. Her wish is soon fulfilled. The royal soldiers, aroused by the statue Sergius has pushed out of the window, cut him down with their fire.

In some ways, *Morgane* is technically superior to Villiers' earlier play. While *Elën* is composed of two virtually separate intrigues, loosely tied together, the subplots in *Morgane* coalesce into a unity. Lady Hamilton's ambition directly threatens the success of Morgane's and Sergius' plans; the feelings Morgane has for Sergius prevent the accomplishment of their goal. Likewise, Sione's infatuation with Sergius ultimately results in the protagonists' downfall.

Furthermore, while some of the dramatic irony in *Elën* (especially the irony involving the flowers) is heavy-handed and awkward, instances of irony in *Morgane* are more consistently subtle. For example, in an attempt to do good by taking Sione to Naples, where she can test the strength of her religious vocation, Morgane does nothing but cause her own misfortune; Sione's presence in Naples permits the encounter with Sergius that convinces Morgane of the veracity of Lady Hamilton's lies. Act IV, in which Lady Hamilton arrives in Morgane's camp, contains the best example of irony in the play. Although it is ostensibly the victorious Morgane who has Hamilton the suppliant in her power, in reality, it is the latter who by her lies exercises dominance over the former. A final irony is that Morgane snatches defeat from the jaws of victory by losing control of herself and her emotions at the precise moment that she has so skillfully gained physical control of virtually every other element in the kingdom.

Moreover, the use of nonverbal techniques to suggest interior qualities of characters is more varied and imaginative in *Morgane* than in *Elën*. Musical motifs are used in both plays. "Gaudeamus," sung by the students in *Elën*, suggests their carefree disposition, whereas the anthem "God save the Queen," which accompanies Lady Hamilton's entrance in Act IV of *Morgane*, calls to mind her English nationality and certain qualities, such as reserve and political shrewdness, associated with that people in the nineteenth century. Only in *Morgane*, however, does Villiers use characters' gestures to reflect their interior realities. The technique is used sparingly (*Corr*, I, 188), but effectively. A brilliant example occurs in Act III, where Morgane and Hamilton, long jealous of each other and now in bitter competition for control of the Two Sicilies, are shown playing a game of chess.

Nevertheless, Villiers did not always avoid flaws evident in his first drama. The instances of implausible motives and unbelievable character are as numerous here as before. Lady Hamilton, who is monomaniacally driven by her hatred of Morgane and her desire to retain political power, lacks any shading to her character and, consequently, any real human fullness. The witch Monna Jahëli is totally unbelievable in the context of the world Villiers creates in the play—a world in which ambition, resolve, tenacity, not magic, determine the course of events. The characters Eaque, Thurn, and San Vaënza, hardly developed, are mere automatons.

In addition, Villiers depends as heavily on coincidence to initiate and develop action as he did in *Elën*. It is totally by chance that Morgane is sent in Act I to the very place that Sergius is held prisoner and, what is more, that the prisoner should happen to have a legitimate claim to the Sicilian throne. It seems contrived in Act IV that Sergius and Sione should pass by Morgane's camp and that Morgane should happen to witness the fatal good-bye kiss they exchange. Similarly, at the end of Act IV, Sergius swoops down out of the blue, arriving just in time to save Morgane from the executioner's block; while in Act V, the nun selected to prepare Morgane for death happens to be Sione, who reveals the truth about Sergius and herself.

Finally, *Morgane* reveals as many (and perhaps more) instances of melodrama as *Elën*. The final act of the play contains so many melodramatic touches that a situation that should be serious becomes ridiculous. Not only does Sergius push a statue out of the cell window, mount its pedestal, and hide himself under a cloth, but Morgane dies a victim of a glove that Lady Hamilton has dipped into poison. The disguise and the outlandish murder weapon are pure conventions of the Romantic melodrama.

C. La Révolte

After writing three short stories, Villiers produced his third drama in 1869. *La Révolte* differs considerably from his two earlier plays, since it consists of only one act, has only two characters, and is set in Paris in the nineteenth century. Most significantly, whereas the early plays were heavily influenced by Romantic dramas, *La Révolte*, which was written to challenge social mores and to reform the French theater, purveyor of those mores and "clown of the other nations" (*OC*, VII, preface, xx), betrays the influence of the social dramas of Alexandre Dumas *fils*.[32] It is understandable, then, that Dumas himself was willing to exercise influence to get this play staged (6 May 1870) and that Villiers dedicated the work to this "dear and illustrious friend" (ix).

In a setting of red, black, and gold, the play opens with Elisabeth at a desk doing calculations and her husband Félix smoking a cigar. Concerned about his wife's health, for "if [she] became sick whom could [he] trust to keep his books" (10), the businessman asks Elisabeth to rest. He tells her that they must get out more; go to the country, for it "inspires fresh, often lucrative, ideas," (10); attend the theater, where "one can run into good deals" (10). When the sound of a carriage is heard, Elisabeth gets up and hands Félix a bag of money. With the wages earned as Félix's bookkeeper, Elisabeth explains, she is buying back her freedom by compensating him for her dowry and living expenses. The idealistic wife can no longer accept a stultifying, materialistic existence and wishes to live, to dream, to "contemplate . . . an occult world of which the exterior realities are scarcely a reflection, . . . to die . . . with a bit of heaven in [her] eyes" (26–27). In spite of Félix's charges that she has lost common sense and is irresponsible in abandoning husband and daughter, Elisabeth leaves in the waiting carriage. Félix falls asleep, muttering reproaches ("She is a bad mother! It is against nature, it is impossible!"[38]) yet already missing his wife ("How stark it is here! I hadn't noticed it" [38]). The clock strikes one o'clock, then two, three, four. Dawn is breaking as a shivering Elisabeth enters. Having realized that she has lived too long under stultifying conditions and cannot be anything but what she has become, she has returned to resign herself to a dutiful and upstanding life with her husband and daughter. Overjoyed to see his wife, the awakened Félix warns that "as long as there is 'poetry' on earth, the lives of upstanding people will not be safe" (45).

It must be admitted that neither of the characters in the play (which reminds one of Henrik Ibsen's *A Doll's House* [1879])[33] is believable. Elisabeth and Félix lack nuance, typify purity of soul and materialistic obsession, and come close to simply embodying abstract principles.[34] More than that, it is evident from the satiric way Villiers treats Félix that his sympathies lie with Elisabeth and that he execrates her short-sighted, materialistic, bourgeois husband. The play is weighted against the latter, and Elisabeth is clearly a spokesman for Villiers' own negative impressions of contemporary bourgeois society and people like Félix. The unfortunate consequence of this is that the drama at times is too preachy, too concerned with conveying a message. Contrary to Villiers' intentions, the audience may even feel more sympathy for Félix, so bitterly flayed by the author's satire, than for the too noble, uncompromising Elisabeth.[35] A final weakness in the play is the melodramatic detail it contains. For one thing, Villiers suggests that Elisabeth may be contemplating suicide, for while talking to her husband she "absent-mindedly plays with a little traveling pistol" (32). Then too, before leaving the house, Elisabeth hands Félix a crystal paperweight which, she self-righteously announces, should forever remind him of the purity of her soul (35–36).

In spite of these weaknesses, there are many good things to say about the play. First, the events in this play, unlike some of those in Villiers' two previous plays, result totally from the psychology of the characters, not from chance happening. Second, Villiers uses irony very subtly in the play. Before announcing dissatisfaction with her husband's values and a desire to leave, Elisabeth says to Félix: "What woman would not be proud of your praises" (7). Moreover, it is at dawn, ordinarily associated with rebirth and revitalization, that Elisabeth arrives home to resume her gloomy and lifeless existence. Third, Villiers' style is varied and suitably adapted to character and situation. While Félix speaks in clipped, economical sentences, the words of the noble Elisabeth rise at times to levels of lyricism, as when she says she wants to "die . . . with a bit of heaven in [her] eyes" (27). Finally, gestures and color are most effectively used to reflect the personality of the characters and the life they lead. Not only is the bourgeois self-contentment of Félix (Latin: happy) suggested by his cigar smoking, but so is Elisabeth's later resignation to life with him by her throwing off the traveling cloak and readjusting her dress before the mirror (43). The black in the decor of the sitting room as well as in Elisabeth's dress suggests the deadly existence the heroine is leading, while the gold in the setting represents money, the very foundation of that existence. The red, on the other hand, symbolizes Elisabeth's thirst for life and freedom.

Villiers' three early dramas display much imaginative experimentation. In these works, he developed themes like the ideal woman and the conflict of ideal and mundane, suggested by his own experiences; he also employed irony, musical motif, gesture, and color very effectively. Nonetheless, the dramas reveal that Villiers was having difficulty in creating believable characters within a historic and realistic framework and in avoiding melodramatic touches. There can be little doubt that, even as late as 1870, "nobility of conception far outstripped his theatrical know-how."[36] Villiers himself seems to have had an intimation of this. Not only did he express disappointment with *Morgane* (*Corr*, I, 83,94), but he was also to rework it later on.

IV *Extant Prose Poems*

The first of the prose poems is about a drunkard who begins to bludgeon his wife and then after the first blow repents. Nevertheless, he realizes that "it was better to finish so she would suffer less, since it was [already] too late after this blow."[37] The theme of the work and the mordant irony suggest a direct imitation of Baudelaire. The other two extant prose poems, on the other hand, display greater originality.

The autobiographical "El Desdichado" ("The Dispossessed"), which is the basis for the later short story "Souvenirs occultes" (*CC*, 277–83), is divided into three stanzas. In the first, Villiers evokes his Breton ancestors, "stock of bizarre warriors" (*CC*, 482), and in particular his grandfather, Jean-Jérôme de Villiers de l'Isle-Adam, who served in India (1786–1789) and gained distinction as a "despoiler of tombs" (482). The second stanza sketches the fate of Jean-Jérôme: His nocturnal expeditions among royal sepulchers came to an end when he fell into an ambush; he died "amid frightful tortures" (483), and his booty was dispersed in caves atop the Himalaya Mountains. In the last stanza, Villiers contrasts himself with his forebear. He has inherited "the dazzling sights of the funereal soldier" (483); but he walks in the dew of dark alleys, whereas Jean-Jérôme walked among the jewels of dark tombs. Like Gérard de Nerval, from whose sonnet (1853) the title of this work is borrowed, Villiers paints himself as someone dispossessed. Nevertheless, unlike Nerval, who sees himself dispossessed primarily of love, Villiers regrets that his century has deprived him of the possibility of attaining the same prestige as his ancestors ("I carry in my soul the sterile riches of a great number of forgotten kings" [483]).

"A celle qui est morose" is more hermetic than "El Desdichado" and at times is quite unclear. The woman of whom it is a question and to whom the prose poem is dedicated is not, as Auriant claims, Villiers' muse, "morose in that bourgeois, fashionable, material, and materialistic century,"[38] but rather a real woman who presumably waylaid Villiers in love. The writer characterizes this woman as a "musician" with the "voice of Armida," a reference to the Circe-like enchantress of Tasso's *Jerusalem Delivered*, who seduced Rinaldo and momentarily distracted him from his high destiny in her fantastic garden.[39] Alluding to the bird associated with love, he also describes her as a "child" who "plays with my thought like the nightingale with night." Finally, he calls her a "svelte vision" and a "very reasonable fairy"; he addresses her as his "fiancée."

The work is based on an introductory remark, a phrase of which is reproduced at the end of each of four stanzas. In the first stanza, Villiers asks his muse to talk about the woman whom he appears to have left ("abandoned arms"). "Formerly," she came to him in her gardens, and her "crystalline laughter disturbed sirens and charmers." The thought of her "hurts deliciously." The next two stanzas evoke the woman as Villiers now imagines her. Her dark hair "rests" upon her "paleness." She is "quiet." Her face appears "sullen," and she looks "seriously" at the waves. The thought of "her eyes filled with veiled prayers" makes him forget "former disillusions" and tempts him once again: "the child plays with my thought." Consequently, in the last stanza, the writer admonishes the woman to stay in "your solitary gardens," where, scornful of pure love ("the faithful lily"), "you shred with your cutting teeth the banal roses" and "talk about your dreams" with shadows ("mystical flowers, censers of shadow").

It is quite obvious that Villiers borrowed the title "A celle qui est morose" from Baudelaire's poem "A celle qui est trop gaie." In addition, Raitt has suggested that Aloysius Bertrand, author of *Gaspard de la Nuit* (1842), exercised a major influence on this work.[40] I think, however, that the major influence on Villiers in writing this prose poem was probably the memory of his own unhappy experience with Louise Dyonnet.

V *First Short Stories*

A. *"Claire Lenoir" and "L'Intersigne"*

Villiers' short story "Claire Lenoir" (1867) is a supposed "mem-
orandum" of a harrowing experience, written in the first person by
Dr. Tribulat Bonhomet. This character is a devotee of astrology,
chiromancy (palmistry), and physiognomy (science of determining
character from facial features), a firm believer in common sense,
science, and material progress, but sceptical of God and the supernatural, in short, the archetypical bourgeois of his century. Aboard a
ship bound for Saint-Malo, where he is to visit his friends the
Lenoirs, Bonhomet meets an English officer, Sir Henry Clifton,
who has been, he suspects, adulterously involved with Mme
Lenoir. The next day, after reading in a Saint-Malo café that the
Paris Academy of Sciences has authenticated a theory that
slaughtered animals retain in their eyes "the impression of the objects they have seen before they die" (Droug, I, 56),[41] Bonhomet is
received into the Lenoir home. The spectacled Claire is not only
partial to Hegelianism but also, as her name implies, sensitive to the
interior light of the Christian religion. Césaire, on the other hand,
believes in the transcendental reality taught by occultism and
Hegelian philosophy but discounts totally his wife's Christianity.[42]
The three discuss music, literature, and philosophy. The materialist
doctor self-contentedly ridicules the music of Wagner, the stories of
Edgar Allan Poe, and occult and philosophical theories, as well as
"sentimental" religious beliefs. Some days later Césaire, who has
long tried to overcome "devouring instincts within [him]" (127), dies
of apoplexy, vowing in a mysterious fashion to take vengeance on
the adulterer.

One year after Lenoir's death, Bonhomet is in the French town of
Digne, where he not only learns that Clifton, the supposed seducer
of Claire, has been decapitated by a Polynesian pirate (Ottysor) but
also meets Mme Lenoir herself, who is now dying, ravaged "by
some mysterious anguish" (144). After acknowledging her past
infidelity with Clifton, the dying woman tells Bonhomet that three
and a half months after her husband's death, Césaire appeared to
her in a dream as an Ottysor. At the point of death, Claire has
another vision, this time of the Ottysor clutching Clifton's severed
head. Remembering the Academy of Sciences' findings concerning
the eyes of dead animals, Bonhomet seizes his ophthalmoscope and

examines the dead woman's eyes. There, refracted in her eyeballs, is the apparition of Césaire-Ottysor holding Clifton's bloody head. Bonhomet, who has always rejected notions of a transcendental reality, is sorely afraid, for his own experiment has empirically proved beyond the shadow of doubt the existence of the apparition and the supernatural.

Villiers' second short story, "L'Intersigne" (1867–1868), is written in the first person from the perspective of a young nobleman, Baron Xavier de la V***. Returning home one night from a spiritualist meeting, Xavier finds himself mortally pale and in low spirits. In the hopes of curing himself, he leaves the horrible worries of Paris for Saint-Maur (Lower Brittany) to visit his old friend Fr. Maucombe, whom he has not seen since the priest's pilgrimage to the Holy Land. Forgetting his cloak in a hotel along the way, the young man arrives the next day at the rectory. In a momentary hallucination, the details of the house (steps resembling tombstones, a nearby graveyard, a knocker resounding like a tolling bell) conjure up to him notions of death. Just before bedtime, the priest's ailing appearance, of which Xavier has been until then unaware, gives him the same sensation of death. During the night, in an attack of lucid somnambulism, the visitor witnesses a prophetic scene. At midnight, the bedroom door opens. A priest, who evinces "a breath of the other world" in the pale moonlight and whose face is indistinguishable, save for two pupils "staring solemnly," holds out a traveling cloak as if to offer it. A night bird flies by (Droug, I, 183). Terrified, Xavier slams and locks the door.

The next morning, before the guest is able to relate fully the supposed "dream" to his host, an urgent letter arrives, and he is forced to return home on business. Accompanied by Maucombe, Xavier sets off for the train. A chilling rain begins to fall. In the pale moonlight, Maucombe bids adieu after first "staring solemnly" at his friend and offering him his traveling cloak just as in Xavier's "dream" of the previous night (191–92). A flock of birds passes overhead and alights on the rectory and church far off in the distance. Troubled by the resemblance between these incidents and his "dream" as well as the portents of death, Xavier is glad to retrieve his own cloak at the hotel, send Maucombe's back to him, leave the "country of nightmares" and "Death," "return into real life," and chalk the whole experience up to "coincidence" (194–95). Back in Paris, Xavier is informed that Fr. Maucombe died at midnight, the

very hour of the "dream," from a cold caught in accompanying his
friend to the train. He was happy to be enshrouded in the cloak that
he had brought back from the Holy Land.

A similarity between these two tales is clear. Structurally, the
original versions of both are first person narratives, divided into
chapters with titles and epigraphs.[43] Thematically, both are concerned with death and what Eliphas Lévi called the sideral or astral
body (second body belonging to each individual through life and
surviving him in death). With his astral body assuming the form of
an Ottysor, Lenoir in death takes revenge on Claire and Clifton,
whereas Fr. Maucombe's astral body appears in the night presumably to warn Xavier of his imminent death. Finally, both tales, with
their "systematic and ruthless evocation of fear" and "cult of the
bizarre,"[44] betray the influence of Edgar Allan Poe's short stories.
Now, the Poe resonances are by no means fortuitous, for Villiers
admitted writing "Claire Lenoir" at least "according to the esthetic
of Edgard [sic] Poe" (*Corr*, I, 99).[45] Moreover, the thematic and
structural resemblance of "Claire Lenoir" and "L'Intersigne" is totally understandable since they were written at about the same time
as the first in a series of tales entitled *Histoires moroses* for publication in the *Revue des Lettres et des Arts*. The journal's motto "Faire
penser" ("To make one think") suggests that the purpose of stories
published therein was to wrench a materialistic society from its common sense smugness and to offer for its contemplation the "simple
possibility" (Droug, I, 32) of supernatural events.

Both tales excel in their great ability to create fear and suspense in
the reader. To provoke these reactions, both rely on many of the
same techniques. For instance, both are told from the perspective of
nervous, excitable men—Xavier by temperament, and Bonhomet
because of the events he has witnessed and is about to recount. The
result is that the language of the tales is highly charged with anxious
emotion. Moreover, the narrators in both stories combine realistic
descriptions of objects and places with their accounts of eerie
events. Portrayal of the mysterious within a realistic framework
induces the reader to accept seriously, almost against his will, the
reality of the frightful events being reported. Then, in "L'Intersigne" and in parts of "Claire Lenoir," the reader hardly has time to
digest and forget one bizarre incident before a new happening un-
nerves him; the narrator offers little solace to the audience, for he is
at a loss to explain anything. Finally, "Claire Lenoir" (as well as the
1883 edition of "L'Intersigne," but not the original) opens by

suggesting the eeriness and incredibility of the story about to be revealed. This not only creates apprehension in the reader but suspense as well. He reads on eagerly to satisfy his curiosity.

The tales also excel in character portrayal. Xavier of "L'Intersigne" is a man interested in supernatural phenomena (hence his attendance at a spiritualist meeting) yet incredulous and fearful in their presence, susceptible to nervous anxieties, young and impulsive (hence his speedy departure from Paris), eager to find solace in the reassuring priest, and relieved when he can flee an uncomfortable situation. On the other hand, Fr. Maucombe is a warm and generous human being who is also capable of reproaching Xavier for not visiting him sooner, a pious and devoted man of God, an intellect and scholar, and an enthusiast of hunting and fishing. Tribulat Bonhomet (in part based on Flaubert's Homais and Henri Monnier's Joseph Prudhomme) is, by his own admission, the archetype of the nineteenth century. Nevertheless, Villiers develops traits in this character (smugness, hate and condescension, stemming from narrow-mindedness, insecurity, and a fear of the unknown) that prevent him from remaining strictly symbolic and give him a rich psychological dimension. Critics generally accept Tribulat's human dimension, but some fault the novel because the other principal characters lack the same human fullness.[46] It is true that in Chapters IX–XII, Claire and Césaire appear as embodiments of abstract philosophical positions, Claire personifying theistic Hegelianism, her husband atheistic Hegelianism. It is also true that in subsequent chapters they appear maniacally driven by a single force, Césaire by revenge and Claire by fear. Yet, these critics fail to remember that the whole story is told from Tribulat's perspective, and it is significant that the materialist is unable to perceive the Lenoirs as human beings.

Despite its simple plot, evocation of fear, and masterful characterization, however, "Claire Lenoir" does not give the same unity of impression, so necessary to the short story, as the later "L'Intersigne." This is true for two reasons. The first reason is the long philosophical discussion by the Lenoirs and Bonhomet in the middle of the story (Chapters IX–XII). While it is indisputable that this discussion adds to one's knowledge of the characters, its extreme length, in my opinion, does more harm than good to the tale as a whole. It interrupts the action, weighs down the story with erudition (gleaned primarily from Eliphas Lévi and Véra's *Introduction à la philosophie de Hegel*[47]), dispels momentarily the atmosphere of

fear, and imposes a dramatic form on an essentially narrative work.
In "L'Intersigne," Villiers wisely curtails these potentially disruptive conversations—Xavier and Fr. Maucombe's religious discussion, for example, is summarized: "We moved from the *Punctum
saliens* to the *Ens realissimum*. Eternal theme of the great human
Dream. / 'To conclude,' Maucombe said to me in getting up, 'We are
here to know' " (Droug, I, 178)[48]—and relies chiefly on description
and action to portray characters.

"Claire Lenoir" is also less unified than "L'Intersigne" because it
fails to sustain a consistent tone throughout the story. By describing
Xavier's hallucination, the nocturnal appearance, the similarity between the apparition and the events the following night, and
Maucombe's death, Villiers maintains an atmosphere of fear, suspense, and mystery to the very conclusion of his tale. On the contrary, the moments of fear and suspense that Villiers creates in
"Claire Lenoir" are dispersed with interludes of humor and satire. It
is clear that Villiers wished not only to scare his reader into contemplating the possibility of the supernatural but also to satirize, in
the person of Tribulat, a certain reigning bourgeois mentality and
"dangerous cultural tendencies" that he feared and abominated.[49]
"The fact is," he wrote to Mallarmé in discussing the tale, "I will do
with the bourgeois, if God grants me life, what Voltaire did with
'clericals,' Rousseau with gentlemen, and Molière with doctors"
(*Corr*, I, 99).

There is no disputing that Villiers has done a masterful job in
satirizing the bourgeois mentality through the person of Bonhomet.
By giving him the narrative perspective Villiers permits the character to indict himself. His pretentious comparisons between the
Quakers, the Lake Poets, King Charlemagne, and himself (Droug,
I, 34–35) point up all the more clearly how immoral, inhumane, and
lackluster Bonhomet and everything he stands for really are. His
profession of faith in progress and the empirical sciences, even the
quasi-sciences of astrology, physiognomy, and chiromancy, is done
so seriously, unquestioningly, and pietistically that it becomes risible. His pedantry, designed to impress us (Chapter VI), has just the
opposite effect and makes us laugh. And his dogmatic stance in
discussion belies his supposed interest in scientific inquiry. Yet,
despite the brilliance of this satire, there is little doubt that it carries
with it a negative effect. It is rarely possible within the confines of
the short story to blend tones without partially destroying unity.

B. *"Azraël"*

Villiers' third short story, "Azraël" (later amplified and titled "L'Annonciateur"), begins with lush, detailed descriptions of Jerusalem, the royal palace, the Hall of Wonders within the palace, and King Solomon enthroned in the hall. The king-seer is surrounded by his minister, Helcias, royal captives, ferocious lynxes, royalty, dancers, and offerings from all the tribes of Israel. This night, the king and his people are commemorating their ancestors' flight from Egypt and the miraculous destruction of the pursuing Egyptian army in the Red Sea. At the sudden appearance of whirlwinds, Helcias advises the frightened court to continue its celebration. Upon deliberation, he realizes that the eddies are being caused by the approach of Azraël, the angel of death. The court is thrown into panic. Some beseech Solomon, thinking his magical powers can save them from Azraël's summons. Others point an accusing finger at the dancers of Nephtali for bringing on this misfortune. Still others chant death songs, certain that their last day has come. The torches grow dimmer, and the royal palace becomes enveloped from bottom to top in heavy mist as Azraël arrives. Feeling that the angel's "torrid" stare upon him has produced no result, Helcias begs Solomon to transport him magically to a "ruined clearing where the Serpent landed the first night of the world" (Droug, I, 237). After he grants Helcias the request, Solomon asks the angel why he has come to court. Azraël responds that he stopped to greet the king, but was surprised to find Helcias there, for he had been sent by the all-knowing God to the "ruined clearing where the Serpent hid himself the first night of the world" (Droug, I, 240) to summon him to death.

It is apparent that "Azraël" differs in form and content from Villiers' two other tales. It is a third person, not a first person, narration; it is not divided, like the early tales, into chapters; and its mellifluous language resembles more that of Villiers' prose poems than the strict prose of "Claire Lenoir" and "L'Intersigne." Moreover, "Azraël," unlike the first stories, is relatively static; very little happens in the narrative. The setting is not nineteenth century Brittany but Israel ten centuries before Christ. And Villiers appears less concerned with causing terror than with evoking the color and feeling of a historical epoch. The influence of Edgar Allan Poe seems to have played a less decisive role in "Azraël" (June 1869) than in the two stories Villiers published almost a year and a half earlier. Far more than Poe's presence, one detects the influence of the Parnassian esthetic—the impersonal depiction of plastic beauty and the cult of formal perfection—that may have rubbed off on Villiers during his collaboration on the *Revue fantaisiste* (1861) and the *Parnasse contemporain* (1866) or from his association with Banville, François Coppée, and José-Maria de Heredia.

Most assuredly, "Azraël" is a work that is not going to appeal to everyone. Its dearth of action, lack of character analysis, quantity of rare words, philosophical erudition, and occasional excesses of stylistic refinement may be bothersome to the modern reader. Several critics have quite rightly, I think, criticized the work on this last account.[50] As for the other criticism, however, it must be remembered that Villiers never intended to write a story of character or action. Rather, his intention was to develop certain philosophical themes and to evoke the colorful history of Israel within the framework of an old Talmudic legend, borrowed from Collin de Plancy's *Les Légendes de l'Ancien Testament* (1861).[51] Keeping his purpose in mind, one has to admit that Villiers has succeeded (despite the occasional tiring lyricism) in creating a tale that displays beautiful local color, meticulous organization, and some interesting philosophical ideas.

There are two principal themes that Villiers treats in "Azraël." The first is death. Dina Lanfredini, in fact, labels the tale a "harmonious, religious poem of death."[52] As Villiers presents it here, death is not the tragic mystery it was in "Claire Lenoir" nor the end of conscious being as described by atheistic materialists. Rather it is considered a beginning and a liberation from the confinement of what we ordinarily call life (Droug, I, 238). The tale implies not only that Helcias flees to the clearing in hopes of meeting his death (236–37), but also that Solomon is sorely disappointed to learn that Azraël has not come to free him from his earthly existence (238). In the character of Solomon, Villiers develops a second theme, suggested to him by occult or Hegelian philosophy.[53] The Solomon depicted in "Azraël" is not simply a monarch of great wealth. He is also and above all the seer, favored by God, who has overcome the limits of his human nature, liberated his soul, and arrived at the highest degree of knowledge, perfection, purity, and power. Villiers had already alluded to the concept of seer in *Isis*, and in later works he would develop this theme as well as the theme of death the liberator.

The tale is artistically noteworthy, however, chiefly because of its formal perfection. It is organized in three parts: a prelude (211–19), a description of Azraël's approach (219–30), and an account of his visit (230–40). Employing in the prelude what we may call an almost cinematographic technique, Villiers first presents the reader with a panorama of Jerusalem, then directs his gaze toward the royal palace, leads him inside the palace to the Hall of Wonders where Passover is being celebrated, focuses his attention on King Solomon, and finally diverts his attention to the people surrounding the king. With its progression from without to within the palace and its account of a religious ceremony, this first part serves not only to describe the tale's setting and to set a solemn tone for the work but also to foreshadow another movement toward the palace, Azraël's gradual approach, treated in the second part. Villiers does not describe this movement directly. Rather, he keeps narrative perspective within the palace and suggests Azraël's advance by describing the increasingly perceptible effects it produces. First, there appear the shadowy whirlwinds (220), caused by the angel's flight. As he comes closer, a flame of a menorah bends toward the crowd, snakes hide, and the royal lynxes become restless (222). Finally, a growing intensity of darkness blots out all torches (230), and Azraël alights on the royal esplanade. In contrast to the movement in the first two parts, movement in the third part is from within the palace to without and away. Not only does Helcias flee the court for the clearing near the Euphrates, but Azraël's imminent departure from the court to the clearing is also strongly suggested at the tale's conclusion.

Besides its careful organization, the tale is also artistically noteworthy for its ability to conjure up a feeling for Israel. Villiers achieves this end, first, by using the Hebraic spelling of certain proper names (Schaül, Hierouschalaïm) and sometimes the Hebrew word instead of the French equivalent (Misraïm for Egypte). Then, as Drougard has already intimated, Villiers introduces into his story of Solomon all of Hebraic civilization, from the serpent to Jesus Christ, by a skillful series of references to important events in the history of Israel (serpent, flood, Egyptian captivity, Saul's rule, slaughter of the innocents, Christ's betrayal in Gethsemane).[54] Moreover, especially in the prelude, Villiers gives lush descriptions of Jerusalem, the royal palace, and the celebrators, noting in detail color, form, texture, sounds, and even smells. For example, he writes: "Adorned with dark fabrics and pearl diadems on their foreheads, the Women of the second class rest on their elbows, in shameless poses, upon purple beds—and, when they inhale their sachets of *besham*, the small silver bells that border the fringe of their sindons jingle" (218–19). Clearly, in this description, Villiers appeals to all senses except taste. Finally, Villiers reinforces description by the onomatopoetic sounds of his prose. Taking but one example, we read: "Ainsi est endormie, sous la solennité des siècles, aux bruits prochains des torrents, la citadelle de Dieu, Sion la Prédestinée" (213).[55] The soft *s* sounds of the first and last parts of the sentence, characterizing a silent Jerusalem, stand in marked contrast to the hard *r* sounds in the words "aux bruits prochains des torrents" that depict noise nearby.

There are several observations to be made about Villiers' first short stories. First, they display great variety; Drougard, in fact, has suggested that they represent "the three principal types of stories Villiers will later cultivate: the satiric tale, the story of mystery, the philosophic and historic prose poem."[56] Second, the tales are not, unfortunately, of the same caliber. The last two, "L'Intersigne" and "Azraël," are not only more concise and tightly structured than "Claire Lenoir," but they also evince, unlike the first tale, a consistent tone, creating in the reader a unity of impression. Finally, although it must be admitted that none of the original versions of Villiers' early stories is without fault—the author himself was aware of this and would rework each of them later—they all nevertheless reveal his incontestable skill in transmitting moods, creating local color, and developing simple plots in a limited number of pages. These tales mark a turning point in his career: After his more or less unsuccessful attempts at poetry, the novel, and the theater, Villiers seems at last to have found a literary genre more suitable to his temperament and talents.

CHAPTER 3

The Years of Struggle

I Abject Poverty, Family Projects, Resistant
Public (1871–1879)

THE death of Mlle de Kérinou on 13 August 1871 had an adverse effect on Villiers' life. From his earliest days, his great-aunt had been virtually the sole support of the family, and since her fortune was tied into annuities, with her death the survivors were left penniless. The burden of supporting the semisenile and reckless Joseph-Toussaint and an aging mother as well as himself fell on Villiers' shoulders. If he was poor before, his existence was now downright precarious. According to Pontavice, the family dwelling had to be given up and the furniture sold. The mother went to the country; father and son separated.[1] Henceforth, Villiers lived day to day without fixed residence, moving from boardinghouse to boardinghouse, from garret to garret.

With the increased responsibility of supporting his parents, Villiers hoped the theater would provide a way to fortune and fame. He wrote L'Evasion in 1871. About the same time, he undertook La Tentation.[2] In October 1872, he published the first part of his drama Axël in the Renaissance littéraire et artistique. Yet, Villiers made no effort to produce L'Evasion until the 1880s, he altogether abandoned work on La Tentation, and he did not complete a first draft of Axël until 1885–1886. Just why the impoverished Villiers did nothing more with these dramas is unclear. It may be that the failure of La Révolte in 1870 discouraged him from staging L'Evasion and from completing the two other dramas. But it may also be that he realized that he had a better chance of selling his short stories than these plays and would have to postpone a triumph in the theater

63

until his financial lot improved. Significantly, from 1873 on, he was composing short stories again.

In December 1873, Villiers journeyed to London in hopes of marrying an Englishwoman named Anna Eyre. There is little doubt that the indigent nobleman was initially interested in her money; a contract between Villiers and a certain Count de la Houssaye, dated 23 December 1873, stipulates that the fortune of the woman whom De la Houssaye introduced and Villiers married "be a minimum of three million" (*Corr*, I, 180). Yet, during his stay, the incurably romantic Villiers appears to have fallen in love; he reported with great emotion to Mallarmé on 5 January 1874 that "I love the only possible wife for me. Her millions, that is fine . . . but it is no longer that at all" (*Corr*, I, 184). Just why these matrimonial plans failed remains mysterious, but two explanations are possible. In a letter to Mallarmé, Villiers suggests that Eyre's father was hostile to the wedding (*Corr*, I, 185); conceivably the father refused to give his daughter in marriage. The theory most often advanced, however, is that Villiers soon realized that Eyre was not at all like the poetic idealization he had of her. A contemporary, John Payne, who met both Villiers and Eyre in London, lends credence to the theory, for he confided to Mallarmé that "the unfortunate result came from the fault of the girl, a young person, rather hysterical and a *poser* (*Corr*, I, 183). Whatever the explanation was, a saddened Villiers returned to Paris in January 1874 and buried himself in work.

Not only did Villiers publish nine more stories by June 1874, but he again tried to have his drama *Morgane* performed (*Corr*, I, 187). When these efforts failed, he decided at year's end to revise the play totally (*Corr*, I, 189). Negotiations to stage the revised version of the play, now called *Le Prétendant*, at the Arts Theater broke down in the spring of 1875, when the theater's director, Emile Weinschenk, left abruptly for America.[3]

At about this time, Villiers entered a writing competition, organized in honor of the forthcoming 1876 American Centennial by the impresario Theodore Michaëlis. No doubt Villiers was as much motivated by the proposed prize of 10,000 francs and a promise to stage the winning play as by the subject matter itself. In April 1875, he left the distractions of Paris for the area near Nantes where, as a guest of Fernand de Gantès, he would be better able to work on his entry, *Le Nouveau Monde*, and probably on further revisions of *Le Prétendant* (*Corr*, I, 197-202).[4]

Soon after his return to Paris in May, Villiers was strolling one evening in front of the Châtelet Theater. He noticed that a revival was playing there of Anicet Bourgeois and Edouard Lockroy's pseudohistoric melodrama *Perrinet Leclerc*, in which his supposed ancestor Jean de Villiers de l'Isle-Adam (1384–1437) was portrayed as a traitor. Incensed by the groundlessness of the allegation and the obvious insult to his family name, Villiers entered a suit on 14 July 1875 against the two directors of the theater, Larochelle and Ritt, to bar further performances of the libelous play. During the next two years, Villiers undertook a vast amount of research in an effort to demonstrate his own filiation with the historical personage and to refute the uncomplimentary charges of the play. On 1 August 1877, the civil court of the Seine handed down a verdict. The judges decided against the plaintiff, because, they reasoned, Jean de Villiers de l'Isle-Adam was by this time in the public domain and could be treated in literature as the authors saw fit; Villiers was forced to pay the courtroom proceedings. Even though Villiers was unable to stop performances of *Perrinet Leclerc* and to clear Jean totally from suspicion, he did gain a limited moral victory. The court, basing its decision on the public domain issue, never questioned, as modern critics have done,[5] the validity of the genealogy Villiers drew up linking himself to the old medieval house of Villiers de l'Isle-Adam. Consequently, Villiers was happy to believe that one of his objectives in undertaking the suit—namely, a public and juridical sanction of his family's genealogical claims—was achieved.[6] His sense of victory must have been heightened when, several weeks after the verdict, a Georges de Villiers des Champs, who had disputed Villiers' right to bear the name de l'Isle-Adam, retracted his claim with profuse apologies. A duel to settle the dispute was canceled when Villiers presented to his adversary the genealogical proofs he had drawn up (*Corr*, I, 224–30).

Unfortunately, Villiers' efforts to have his dramas performed did not turn out as well as his legal dispute. When by August 1876 he was still unable to get *Le Prétendant* staged, he accepted the offer of Godefroy d'Herpent (alias Jules de Clerville), man of letters, director of the periodical *Le Spectateur*, friend of Fernand de Gantès, to "work on the definitive execution of this play and hasten its performance as much as he could."[7] Work on *Le Prètendant*, however, was abandoned for reasons that are still not entirely clear. What is known is that sometime after 1876 a dispute developed between

Villiers and his collaborator. A document requiring the latter to pay damages, presumably for not fulfilling the obligations of his contract with Villiers, has survived.[8] So ended Villiers' hope of seeing his work, conceived as *Morgane* twenty years earlier, performed during his lifetime.

Attempts to stage *Le Nouveau Monde* met with no greater success. Although the play received second honors, along with Armand d'Artois and Gabriel Laffaille's *Un Grand Citoyen*, in the Michaëlis competition—no first prize was awarded—the contest settlement, sometime after 22 January 1876, made no stipulation for its production (*Corr*, I, 207–209). In February, the director of the Ambigu Theater, M. Hostein, consented to stage it, but Villiers preferred to withdraw the work when the director of the theater was changed (August 1876). In February 1877, a new director at the theater, L. P. La Forêt, showed some interest in the play, but presumably not enough (*Corr*, I, 222), for in August, right after the *Perrinet* decision, Villiers left Paris for the Bordeaux area, where his cousin Robert du Pontavice was vacationing, with the clear intent of premiering *Le Nouveau Monde* in the old Guyenne capital. During the two months' sojourn with Pontavice, Villiers read his drama to the director of the Grand-Théâtre of Bordeaux—Pontavice gives a most amusing account of the meeting[9]—and began negotiations for its performance. Several months later, however, Villiers was back in Paris, and, "seduced by the fair promises of [Henri] Chabrillat, at that time reorganizing the Ambigu, he withdrew his piece from the director of the Bordeaux theatre, to confide it to this suddenly arisen literary Barnum."[10] Talks with Chabrillat likewise would fail.

After repeated failure to get *Le Prétendant* and *Le Nouveau Monde* performed, Villiers of necessity turned his attention to other projects. For one thing, he continued writing short stories. Seven new ones, including "Le Chapeau chinois" (*Corr*, I, 239–46), appeared between 1875 and 1879; three historical tales ("Hypermnestra," "Isabeau de Bavière," "Lady Hamilton") were also written around this time but not published until after Villiers' death.[11] In addition, he revised and reprinted seven stories that had already appeared and began negotiations with Calmann-Lévy to have his stories published in book form. To his discredit, the publisher rejected the manuscript on 30 October 1877 because "the pieces . . . are less short stories than *articles of a certain kind* or psychological essays and literary fantasies. . . , [and] would not perhaps have a great chance of success with our readers" (*Corr*, I, 237–38). Villiers also began revising "Azraël" for a deluxe edition with etchings by Frédéric Chevalier. Richard Lesclide, the editor, lost patience with the project, however, when Villiers could not decide on a definitive reading; the edition, except for one working copy, never appeared (*Corr*, I, 257). Finally, sometime between 1877 and 1878, Villiers began work on the novel *L'Eve future*, a first version of which would not be completed until 1879 or 1880 (*Corr*, II, 277–78).

With only the meager revenues from his short stories and possibly from odd jobs,[12] Villiers' existence became more and more deplorable. In 1878, as in 1874, he tried to solve his financial difficulties by marrying a woman of wealth. In all likelihood, the idea of pursuing this widow named de Solsona was proposed to Villiers by his eccentric father; as usual the entire family took great interest in the outcome. Villiers' mother, for instance, informed her son that "the young Spanish widow who has more than 90 million is 26 years old, was married at 15, and since she lost her husband, grief, people believe, has fallen upon her bosom." Noting that the widow "received the order from the doctor to go to Nice until January," and indeed "has gone there before coming to Paris with her aunt the duchess," Mme Villiers closed the letter with this cautious advice: "You could indeed join her there, but she is too ill at the moment. I will keep you informed" (*Corr*, I, 251–52). Presumably writing to his father a bit later, Villiers expressed confidence in a happy ending to his labors: "Be calm; I will succeed. Everything is settled; I am sure of success" (*Corr*, I, 253). Despite Villiers' confidence, plans to marry the Spanish widow did not succeed, and in the following year (1879), he was in hot pursuit of another rich woman. Little is known of these plans except that they too evaporated when Villiers learned that Mlle E. . . "has a lover, an important Parisian banker, who *does not want to marry her*" and that "it is no longer a question of [gaining] millions since she has the lover and there is no longer [a way] to marry her" (*Corr*, I, 271). So Villiers' pitiful situation continued.

Robert du Pontavice, who returned from Bordeaux in 1879 and spent a great deal of time with Villiers that year, has left a vivid picture of his cousin's living conditions. "In 1879," he wrote, "Villiers inhabited a room in a furnished hotel in the Rue des Martyrs. . . . Chance had made us neighbours, for I was living at the corner of the Rue Rochechouart and the Rue de Maubeuge. . . . As to the poet's room, it was just as commonplace as might have been expected in a tenth-rate furnished lodging-house."[13] After describing how Villiers' friends tried to provide for him, taking care not to wound his aristocratic pride, Pontavice went on to say: "I got into the habit of going to see him between three and four o'clock in the afternoons. I generally found him sitting up in bed, supported by several pillows, hard at work. . . . Towards six o'clock, and by dint of persecution, I contrived to drag him from between the sheets, and out we went into the streets."[14] Coming to the cafés on the Boulevard Montmartre, Villiers pointed out to Pontavice the money lenders and those sham artists who unashamedly stole the ideas he had imprudently talked about in their presence. "After these walks, Villiers often came and shared the simple dinner which my Breton cook used to prepare for me; and this made a change for him from the indescribable and poisonous eating-house stews on which he was in the habit of feeding."[15] On clear nights, they would spend time on Pontavice's balcony, dreaming; sometimes Villiers would recite from his works. Then, they "would re-enter the drawing-room, and Villiers, still shivering with the excitement of inspiration, would rush to the piano, and, striking some powerful chords, would begin with the full strength of his voice the magnificent choral invocation in the first act of 'Lohengrin.' "[16] Pontavice concluded by praising Villiers' voice, his talents at the piano, and his purported musical compositions, which, unfortunately, were never collected.[17]

Toward 1879, Villiers was a bit of a legend. For some, he was an indigent but brilliant talker, who enraptured café goers with the mellifluous flow of words. For others, he was a chaser of fortunes. For still others, he was an eccentric aristocrat who had waged a long legal campaign to establish his filiation with the house of Villiers de l'Isle-Adam and to clear his ancestor of allegations of treason. For everyone who knew his name, he was a strange and unique character. His talents as a writer, however, were practically unknown to all.[18] The works he published or performed before 1871 were now forgotten. Moreover, despite the productive period between 1871–1879—even in the face of abject poverty and a long legal dispute—Villiers published no book in this period nor staged any play. The seventeen short stories he did publish after 1871 appeared in short-lived periodicals, not well-known to the general public, and were in any event "not sufficient to give an accurate idea of his talents."[19] If Villiers had any reputation before 1879, it was a result of his personality, not his literary accomplishments.

II *Middle Dramas*

Even though *L'Evasion*, *Le Prétendant*, and *Le Nouveau Monde* were not performed before 1879, it is certain that Villiers wrote the three plays as we have them today between 1871 and 1879. One can then look upon them as Villiers' middle plays, coming as they do after his experiments with the theater in 1865–1870 but preceding final work on his dramatic masterpiece *Axël* in the late 1880s.

A. L'Evasion

L'Evasion (1871) is a one act play about a convict named Pagnol, who escapes around 1840 from the prison of Rochefort, where he has been serving a life sentence. Before fleeing across the border, he will help an old man, Mathieu, who is aiding his escape, rob a dowry from a pair of newlyweds, Marianne Lebreuil and Lucien Dumond. After entering the house where the couple is to reside, killing Marianne's old nurse and blocking her bedroom door with a sofa, Pagnol hides behind curtains and waits to learn from the newlyweds where the money is. Blissfully happy, the two enter and voice pity for the escaped prisoner, less fortunate than they. Lucien tells Marianne he is carrying the dowry because "he would have had to leave [her]" to give it to the notary (*OC*, VII, 68). Marianne senses, for reasons unknown, they are "in great peril" (68–69). Overcome by a drug Mathieu put in their wedding meal, they fall asleep on the sofa. Pagnol now has a pang of conscience. He cannot take the money from innocent people. Moreover, although he hears the arrival of the police in the background, he is unable to kill the sleeping couple to permit his flight. Pagnol throws down his knife, crosses his arms, and stoically accepts recapture and the execution that awaits him. "It is funny!" he says, "but. . . it seems to me that it is now I am escaping" (78).

As the last line of the play, as well the epigraph from St. John 11:43, "Lazare, veni foras" ("Lazarus, come forth"), clearly suggests, the subject of this drama is the moral resurrection of a convict. Fallen prey in the past to an illegitimate love (60), Pagnol is redeemed by the example of the pure and selfless love of the newlyweds. It seems fairly certain, as Palgen endeavors to show, that this subject was suggested by Victor Hugo's *Les Misérables* (1862), a mammoth novel about the moral regeneration of the convict Jean Valjean.[20] Unlike Hugo's novel, however, the story here seems a bit improbable, for Pagnol's transformation is much too sudden. At the play's beginning, the convict has ruthlessly killed the old nurse; a few scenes later, at the mere sight of the innocent newlyweds, he refuses to steal from them and is willing to be captured and executed rather than inflict any injury whatsoever upon them.

The rapid transformation of Pagnol is not the only difficulty with the play. For one thing, Villiers never makes it clear why it should be at all necessary for Pagnol to kill the sleeping Lucien and Marianne in order to escape. Could he not simply have moved the sofa blocking the exit without even waking them, especially since the couple has been drugged? For another thing, it seems too arranged that just before danger strikes, the old nurse should wish the house had a watchdog (62) and that Marianne should feel herself in great peril just before she succumbs to the drug. Similarly, it is too neatly arranged that the signal indicating an escaped prisoner should sound just after Lucien and Marianne have entered the house (67), that they should pray for him, and that Pagnol should witness this tender scene from behind the curtains (69). For a third thing, the play borders on bathos in the scenes where the newlyweds demonstrate their affection for one another and where Pagnol proclaims his admiration for the innocent couple.

Critics have been quick to point out these psychological weaknesses in Pagnol's character, his unexplained actions, the neat coincidences in plot, and the sentimentality.[21] Not enough has been said, in my opinion, about the merits of the drama. In the first place, Villiers has done some interesting things with language. During most of the play, he has the convict speak a language that reflects popular pronunciation and grammar. For instance, Pagnol elides vowels ("J'sais pas c'qu'y m'ont fait" [72]) and pronounces *ils* like *y* [i] instead of [il] (Les petits bourgeois l'auraient traitée comme un chien, maintenant qu'y sont heureux" [63]).[22] Moreover, he deletes the negative particle *ne* ("J'les tuerai pas" [75]) and occasionally omits subject pronouns ("Voyons, s'agit pas d'ça" [73]; "Gn'y a que cette porte" [74]).[23] In the last moments of the play, however, Pagnol's speech, as in the words "Il me semble que c'est maintenant que je m'évade" (78)[24], reflects a certain preciousness. Palgen criticizes Villiers for his inconsistency in placing a refined turn of expression in the mouth of a character who has already demonstrated a more common way of speaking.[25] Yet this critic failed to realize that Villiers was trying to suggest the character's inner, spiritual transformation by the very language he used. Granted this change comes about much too abruptly, it is nevertheless artistically satisfying that Pagnol's brutish language be transformed into a noble one as his sense of morality is raised from one reflecting the law of the jungle to a more humane one based on respect and love.

Moreover, *L'Evasion* deserves attention for the ideas it presents. The play is clearly based on an opposition between earthly and spiritual love. Pagnol's life, based as it has been on a love of the flesh (60), money (52), and self (60), stands in marked contrast to the simple, chaste life of the newlyweds. Villiers' faith in the power and value of spiritual love is affirmed not simply because this love protects the young people from harm but also because its example succeeds in conquering their would-be assailant's earthly desires and transforms his life. Villiers' intense disdain for the bourgeois class, hostile to all things spiritual, is likewise made clear. While the hardened Pagnol is unable to rob or murder Lucien and Marianne precisely because their faces reveal the beauty of their love, he would be not at all inhibited if they showed themselves less noble, if their faces revealed bourgeois values, or if their money were neatly piled away. "Still if [only] they were good bourgeois," he laments, "very fat, with their bellies well cared for. . . . Still, if [only their money] were in a secretary with drawers [and] locks!" (71).

B. Le Prétendant

The plot in *Le Prétendant* differs from the plot in the 1866 version entitled *Morgane*. Although Act I, in which Morgane meets and liberates Sergius, is substantially the same in both, Acts II, III, and IV are somewhat different. In Act II of *Le Prétendant*, unlike the early version, Morgane's goddaughter Sione has for a long time renounced any love for Sergius and resolved to enter a convent; through her, we learn that Morgane's rival, Lady Hamilton, once met Sergius and fell in love with him. Scene 9, in which the conspirators discuss their reasons for joining the plot against Ferdinand, is completely new. In the new version of Act III, before Lady Hamilton, disguised as a witch, predicts Sergius' fortune, she reveals to the audience her love for him by exclaiming: "Ah! my hand will not tremble in touching his!" (*LP*, 130). After the prediction,

Sergius recognizes her behind the disguise. Unlike *Morgane*, where Sergius and the conspirators withdraw after the king refuses to duel with his rival, Act III of *Le Prétendant* ends with Ferdinand's departure, surrendering the palace to the insurgents, Sergius' speech evoking the ideal realm he will institute, and the rebels' cheers acclaiming the new king. In Act IV, instead of the witch Monna Jahëli, it is Lady Hamilton who comes to Sergius' tent; she wishes to replace Morgane both as Sergius' lover and as leader of the plot. Rebuffed by him, she goes to Morgane's tent, where she induces her rival to believe Sergius is only using her to gain the throne for Sione and himself. As proof, she directs Morgane's attention to a farewell scene between the two, about which she has known in advance (158–60).

Act V of *Le Prétendant* has been entirely recast. Morgane and Sergius, apprehended by royal forces, are to be executed, for reasons of secrecy, in a convent at Salerno. Morgane is brought in. By chance, the nun chosen to prepare her for death is Sione; she persuades Morgane that there is nothing between Sergius and herself. Lady Hamilton then enters. She offers Morgane the possibility of saving herself by choosing exile. Realizing this is a trick to convince Sergius of her infidelity (199), Morgane refuses, proclaiming defiantly: "In a while his soul and mine will embrace each other in the night" (202). After she is led off, Sergius is brought in. Lady Hamilton offers him exile with her, provided he "deny all [his] ancestry, renounce all [his] rights, declare [himself] an imposter and incendiary" (207). Sergius likewise refuses. Being unable to persuade either Morgane or Sergius to accept exile, Hamilton consents to reunite them before death. However, one of the conspirators, disguised as a monk, enters with Morgane, binds Hamilton, and announces that the people of Naples have taken up Sergius' cause and will soon be there to free him. It will, however, be too late. The royalist officer San Vaënza, accompanied by the king's dragoons, appears and draws fire. Amid distant shouts of "Long live King Sergius! Long live Queen Morgane of Sicily," the lovers fall, glad to accept exile in death (217–19). The drama ends as a chorus of nuns intones the mournful "Miserere, Miserere!" ("Have pity, have pity, O Lord!").

It is not difficult to see that *Le Prétendant* is vastly superior to the first version of the play. In terms of plot, certain gratuitous happenings have been eliminated. No longer is it by chance that in Act

IV Morgane sees Sergius take leave of Sione; Lady Hamilton, who has known in advance of Sione's departure, now designedly directs Morgane's attention to the scene (174–75). Sergius' arrival in Act V is no longer a bolt from the blue; rather, he too has been captured, and he too is led in to be executed (203). Certain melodramatic touches have, moreover, been deleted. Not only has the role of the witch Monna Jahëli been significantly reduced—only a few references to her now being retained (120, 122, 130)—in addition, Morgane does not fall victim to a poisoned glove, early allusions to such a death have been removed, and Sergius neither arrives through a window nor hides under a cloth in the last act. Furthermore, the plot has been reshaped to make it more dramatic and more tragic. Unlike Act III of *Morgane*, where Sergius sheepishly withdraws from the palace, Act III of *Le Prétendant* ends with his triumph: He forces King Ferdinand from the palace and announces plans to establish the ideal kingdom. As a result of this modification in Act III, the first three acts of the play, constituting an ascending action, build to the climatic moment of victory, whereas the last two acts, forming a descending action, reveal the manner by which victory slips through the protagonists' hands. Already in the opening scenes of Act IV, where the rebels are looting, one senses the unbreachable gulf between Sergius' aspirations and existential reality, one foresees his ultimate defeat.

Besides improvements in plot, dramatic irony has been intensified. In addition to the scene in Act IV, where the seemingly all-powerful Morgane falls prey to the insinuations of a seemingly powerless Lady Hamilton, the new version includes two additional scenes grounded in the same irony. One is Act V, scene 7, in which Lady Hamilton concedes that Morgane's "indignant head was still commanding and it will always seem . . . she was the one being obeyed" (202), even though it is Morgane being held prisoner by Hamilton. The other is Act V, scene 10, where D'Assunta binds Hamilton, who all the while protests that "you are the one in my hands even though I am attached to this pillar" (211). In *Le Prétendant*, moreover, the lovers are killed at the precise moment they have acquired an earthly following (219).

Le Prétendant also displays improvements in characterization, the most obvious being Lady Hamilton. In the new version, she appears a far more dominant character; she virtually subsumes the role of

Monna Jahëli, is not absent from Act V as in the original version, and is instrumental in the deaths of the hero and heroine. Even more than that, in *Le Prétendant*, she seems a more interesting and possibly a more credible character. While in the old version she is monomaniacally driven by ambition and an overwhelming desire to maintain power and thwart her rival, here she is motivated by a real love of Sergius and understandable jealousy of Morgane, the woman whom Sergius adores. Another improvement is with the conspirators. No longer are they simply a band of adventurers; in the new version, thanks to the addition of Act II, scene 9, where the conspirators discuss their political beliefs, a deeper psychological dimension has been infused into their characters. Besides ambition, they are now motivated by moral and humanitarian considerations. Then too, three heretofore undeveloped characters, Major Eaque, the count of Thurn, and San Vaënza, have been consolidated into one.[26] The resultant character, San Vaënza, is more interesting than any of the three and takes on special significance in the last act, where, torn as he is between an admiration for the conspirators and a sense of obedience to his orders, he holds the fate of Morgane and Sergius in the balance.

Finally, *Le Prétendant* is superior to *Morgane* because of the rich political and philosophical themes it develops. While the conspirators in *Morgane* seem to lack a political program, their counterparts in the second version discuss their beliefs (93–100). Count Ricci, for instance, is a royalist, wanting only to replace Ferdinand with a new king. On the other hand, Count Ettore de Montecelli expresses both the desire to destroy old régimes and a general disillusionment with all forms of government. In the new version, Sergius outlines plans for an ideal government (146–47). Not only will this government not oppress its people ("I will not make burdens heavier on your shoulders" [146]), it will also subsidize artists ("I want to invite here, to Naples, . . . those . . . who carry torches of Thought, Learning, and Liberty" [147]). It may be, as Castex and Raitt suggest, that the ideas expressed by Montecelli and Sergius were Villiers' very own and that they were influenced by his involvement in the Commune and his admiration for Wagner's patron Louis II of Bavaria.[27] The conflict between love and earthy ambition is a theme in both *Morgane* and *Le Prétendant*. Nevertheless, the idea that true union between lovers is possible only after liberation from material constraints in death is more fully developed in *Le*

Prétendant. There is only one reference to this theme at the end of *Morgane* (*OC*, VIII, 193–94), whereas in the new version there are at least three (*LP*, 200–202, 209, 215–17). Moreover, the end of *Le Prétendant* makes it clear that Sergius and Morgane voluntarily accept their death to effect a perfect union. No doubt it was the influence of Wagner's *Tristan und Isolde,* better known to Villiers after his trips to Germany, that induced him to develop the theme.

In the final analysis, it must be admitted that some chance happenings, such as Sione's unexpected appearance in Act V (189), and certain melodramatic touches, like Leone's change of allegiance (76–77) and the blood-red wine (89), do persist in the new version of the play. Nonetheless, *Le Prétendant* is a great piece of theatrical art. It seems a shame that it went unplayed during Villiers' lifetime and was not published or performed until 1965.

C. Le Nouveau Monde

The first act of *Le Nouveau Monde* (1875) takes place in 1774 at Swinmore, the estate of Lord Lionel Raleigh Cecil, in the English county of Cumberland. Cecil's wife, Lady Ruth, and her ward and confidante, Mary Mark Ellis, are listening to plaintive adieux sung by French colonists as they depart for the New World. Both women are saddened by the music and thoughts of America: Ruth, because her childhood sweetheart Stephen Ashwell, whom she continues to love despite her *mariage d'obéissance* to Lord Cecil, is in Virginia; Mary, because the man she loves, Henri de Vaudreuil, is setting sail for America that very night. Before leaving for the insurgent colonies where he will serve as military governor, Lord Cecil arrives to grant his unhappy wife the divorce she requests and freedom to enter a convent. The ceremony is interrupted, however, by a veiled Mistress Andrews, the former Edith Evandale, who has come from her home in Mount Vernon, Virginia. In order to prevent any possible future union of Ruth with Stephen, the man she too loves, Mistress Andrews arouses Cecil's jealousy by falsely claiming the freed woman's intention is to join her childhood sweetheart (not a convent); she prevails upon him to suspend the divorce. Ruth fears that the misguided Cecil will try to take revenge on Stephen once he arrives in America. To forewarn him, she and Mary join Vaudreuil and his crew, bound for Virginia. Act I ends with the sounds of plaintive adieux, already heard at the opening.

The rest of the drama is set in America. Act II takes place in

Yorktown, where Mistress Andrews, having rapidly crossed the Atlantic, is awaiting the arrival of Ruth, Mary, and Vaudreuil. To
prevent Ruth from meeting Stephen, she plans to kidnap her, with
help from a servant, Moscone, and his old friend, Bob Upfill, and
send her to Lord Cecil, already in Boston. The song of French
sailors announces the ship's arrival. On landing, Ruth and Mary go
to rest. In the meantime, Vaudreuil is met by Stephen himself,
whom George Washington has dispatched to welcome the French
volunteers. Suddenly Mary rushes in, shouting that Ruth has been
kidnapped. A naval combat ensues; Ruth is saved by Stephen and
Vaudreuil.

Act III takes place in Mount Vernon, near Yorktown, in 1775.
Mary and Vaudreuil have been married. Ruth, who has not told
Stephen that she is still married to Lord Cecil, continues to reject
his proposals. There is talk of revolution in the air. Mistress Andrews coaxes Moscone, whom the purity of American life has temporarily reformed, to aid her in a new plan. She is no longer interested in Ruth's death; she now wants Stephen to despise her
(OC, VII, 190). After a scene between Ruth and Mistress Andrews,
in which the former does not recognize the veiled woman of Act I,
Stephen again asks his beloved why she will not marry him. The
stage now becomes full of colonists; a public meeting has been called
to discuss the tyrannical acts of the British crown. Tom Burnett at
first advises obedience to royal orders since insurrection would hurt
business (205–206) but ends up refusing to pay taxes when a wave of
collectors descends upon him. Stephen, in turn, informs the assembly that Lord Cecil has permitted a massacre in Boston, the Mas-
sachusetts colony is in arms, and one colony after another is finding
peace impossible. Suddenly, British soldiers try to arrest the rab-
ble-rouser. They themselves, however, are prevented by George
Washington and his troops. Praises of liberty and the homeland ring
out. The curtain falls as the populace intone a hymn and the evening
star appears.

Act IV is set in Rhode Island, where Washington's troops, accompanied by Ruth and Mistress Andrews, are planning an attack
against the British. Unbeknownst to all, Mistress Andrews has dis-
closed the whereabouts of the Americans to Lord Cecil, who is
to surround the outpost in an hour's time. After a narration of the
Evandale family history—Mistress Andrews' ancestor Ralph
stabbed his father for marrying a girl he himself loved; the dying

man imprinted his bloody hand on the son's face; and a hand has subsequently reappeared on the faces of all descendants at the moment of death—Washington and Benjamin Franklin enter. The former reveals to Stephen that Ruth is the wife of the British governor and insinuates that she has been acting as an enemy agent. Out of duty, Stephen binds his beloved. No sooner has Washington departed for Dorchester than the remaining colonial troops, under Stephen and Vaudreuil, are attacked by Lord Cecil and his men. In a skirmish, Stephen is wounded and led off by Vaudreuil. Cecil, on the other hand, reaches the rebel camp and unbinds his wife. Taking her up, he gives orders to abandon the forest, ignited by Mistress Andrews, and proceed to Boston.

Act V, set in Boston during the early morning of 4 July 1776, opens with the British generals discussing whether to abandon the city. Lord Cecil hopes the fleet will arrive in time to buttress sagging defenses and beat back Washington's attacking troops. In any event, he himself will fulfill, "up to the end, the mandate [the king] had placed upon [him]" (302): He will never abandon his post. Although he knows he is to die, he momentarily dreams of beginning a new life with Ruth in England. The death of Generals Clinton, Hartley, and Cornwallis is announced, however, and he exits to take command of the remaining troops. Mistress Andrews now enters and threatens to kill Ruth so that "Stephen will at least share [her] despair" (313). As the orchestra plays "The Legend of Ralph Evandale," light falls on the extended hand of a statue of King George III and casts its shadow upon Mistress Andrews' face. Her moment of death, as the legend claimed, has arrived: Dahu, a Indian maiden befriended by Ruth, shoots an arrow into her heart. The wounded Cecil staggers in and falls at the foot of the statue of his king. As Stephen acclaims his military greatness, Ruth removes her wedding ring and places it on the dead governor's finger. The play fittingly ends at dawn with the appearance of George Washington and a proclamation that "the New World is free" (327).

It is obvious to the student of American civilization that inaccuracies abound in this work. Boston, for example, did not surrender to the colonial forces on 4 July 1776. Washington, in fact, was not even in the city on that day. It is unlikely that the septuagenarian and gout-ridden Benjamin Franklin could visit battlefields, and it is fairly certain he was not in Rhode Island between 1775 and 1776. Moreover, it was James Cecil, not Raleigh Cecil as Villiers claims, who was "a considerable personality of this period" (85). He was not, however, like Villiers' character, military governor of the colonies or commander of the royal troops defending Boston.[28] Furthermore, while Clinton and Cornwallis were British generals fighting in America, they were in the New York vicinity, not New England, on the day independence was declared. Finally, palm trees do not grow in Virginia as Act III presumes, and Yorktown is more than "several leagues" from Mount Vernon and not "very close" to Fredericksburg (141). In all fairness, however, the play ought not to be faulted because of such imprecision. Villiers did not claim to be a historian of the American Revolution. As he implies in the preface, it was never his purpose to write a drama of strict historical accuracy. Rather, as a creative mind, he freely adapted facts and events to suit the "overall impression [he] wished to leave" his viewers (84).[29]

What were Villiers' intentions in creating this work? In strict adherence to the rules governing the contest for which he was writing the play, Villiers first wanted to create a personal or "intimate drama" amid the events of 4 July 1776 (83). The major intrigue of the play is not the birth of the nation, but the conflict in Ruth between love for Stephen and duty owed her husband and the eventual triumph of love, notwithstanding moral obstacles and Mistress Andrews' jealousy. The inability of Lord Cecil to retain his wife's love adds a tragic note to the drama, for, despite his royalist allegiance, he is just as noble and admirable as Ruth and Stephen. Not unlike the characters in the dramas of Pierre Corneille (1606–1684), each of the three principal protagonists is motivated by idealism and an inflexible sense of duty. Ruth, for instance, "did [her] duty" in sacrificing love and marrying Lord Cecil (100); she remains faithful to him until his death. Cecil reminds the British generals that his and their "duty is to resist to the last moment" the advancing Americans (301). Finally, when Stephen is asked whether he would sacrifice Ruth's love if it conflicted with his duties as a patriot, he responds unhesitantly and in typically Corneillian fashion: "Ah! if I answered no, would I be worthy of her?" (159).

Although Villiers wished to create an intimate work, he also intended his *Nouveau Monde* to be a "symbolic drama" (84). It was his intention that individual protagonists represent by their traits or words something more than themselves. For example, in the character of Lord Cecil, peer of the realm, friend of George III, and colonial governor, he embodied "the principle of Royalism, as [he] incarnated in Stephen Ashwell," the humble freeman, "the principle of Liberty" (85). On the other hand, Ruth Moore, legally married to an Englishman but partially divorced, bearing a British title but not strictly British—Mary says to her in Act I: "Our country, you well know, is Ireland" (101)—is the "personification of the American earth at this time, earth still half divorced from England, still half free" (86). The legendary Mistress Andrews represents the dark forces of the Old World, "the dark reflection of feudality" (85), while Tom Burnett, the innkeeper who reminds everyone that "time is money" (205), symbolizes materialism.

Because these characters represent ideas, their individual actions take on special significance. The unwillingness of Cecil (representing royalism) to grant a divorce to his wife (representing America), for instance, personifies the crown's refusal to give independence to the colonies. The rivalry between Stephen (i.e., liberty) and Cecil over Ruth represents in miniature the battle being waged by the armies of royalism and freedom for dominance on the American continent. On the other hand, Ruth's conflict between a love for Stephen and a duty to Cecil that lasts until the latter's death personifies the conflict of America herself, torn until the final moment of victory between a desire for freedom and a nostalgic respect for the king. On a more abstract level, Mistress Andrews' near success in capturing Ruth (i.e., America), depriving her of life with Stephen (i.e., liberty), and killing her symbolizes the capability of Old World prejudices and corruption to conquer the New, deprive it of freedom, and even extinguish its newborn life. The attempt by Tom Burnett, the consummate materialist, to dominate the Mount Vernon public assembly suggests a second force, an indigenous materialism, ready to subvert the democratic ideals of the New World. Through his symbolism, then, Villiers succeeds in weaving within the fabric of a personal drama suggestions of both the political battle for independence against which the play is set and the greater but less perceivable metaphysical battle being waged by forces of good and evil for ultimate control in the New World.

Three additional aspects of the play must be noted. Although Villiers made use of music in *Elën, Morgane,* and *Le Prétendant,* its use in *Le Nouveau Monde* was far more elaborate. Song and choruses intervene from time to time in the play. The chanting of adieux at the play's opening, for instance, creates a melancholic

mood that prevades Act I and suggests the sadness of Ruth and
Mary, already "two exiles" in their home at Swinmore (102). After
the colonists defy the British troops by liberating Stephen, they
express their newfound sense of freedom by singing a psalm from
Luther, another rebel who proclaimed his freedom many years ago
(234). In Act II, the arrival at Yorktown of the French ship carrying
Ruth, Mary, and Vaudreuil is heralded by sounds of the crew in the
distance singing an old popular sailing song (159–60). More
significantly, an orchestra is used to comment upon the action of the
play. Musical motifs are associated with characters and ideas; the
orchestra announces these motifs in an overture (97) and recalls
them throughout the work. Lest the audience forget the significance
of his character, Cecil's appearance on stage is accompanied by the
royalist anthem "God Save the King" (107, 325). In like fashion,
"The Ballad of Ralph Evandale," associated with Mistress Andrews,
is intermittently sounded to recall her ominous background and to
suggest her pernicious influence on the events of the play (97, 194,
250, 319). The patriotic song "Hail Columbia!", associated with
America, accompanies Vaudreuil's description of the New World
(132), the death of Andrews and triumph of Ruth, who symbolizes
America (322), as well as the victorious arrival of Washington, father
of the country (326).

Moreover, while *La Révolte* contained a scene with no action or
sound save a clock striking the hour, the extensive use in *Le
Nouveau Monde* of tableaux—scenes with posed characters and little sound, resembling paintings—was new to Villiers' theater. A
tableau precedes the first scene of each of the five acts. In Act I,
Ruth and Mary are "seated" in the manor at Swinmore (92). Bob
Upfill "is asleep" in King George's Tavern at the beginning of Act II
(138). Act III opens with a tableau of a clearing not far from
Stephen's house in Mount Vernon (179). The outpost of the colonial
army with Mistress Andrews "sitting" at a table and "cutting ban-
dages" is depicted in Act IV (235). A tableau in Act V shows Cecil
"standing" and his generals "sitting" at a table in the governor's
mansion (299). The static tableau then comes to life, as the first
scene of each act begins. There are three additional tableaux in the
play. One, depicting a naval battle, is formed in the middle of Act II
(172). In Act IV, there is a tableau representing a forest fire (294);
here, however, the characters talk and move. The play comes to an
end with George Washington, beneath a rising sun, surrounded by

representatives of the New World—Ruth, Stephen, Vaudreuil, Quakers, Indians—and the dead or enchained representatives of the Old—Mistress Andrews, Cecil, Bob Upfill, Moscone (326).

A final aspect of *Le Nouveau Monde* that merits attention is its rich mixture of tones. While examples of irony—as when Stephen says to Mistress Andrews that he pities her for loving unrequitedly, little knowing that he is the object of her affection and the cause of her affliction (238), or when Cecil, at the point of death, thinks there is a possibility of starting a new life with Ruth (306–308)—have ample precedents in Villiers' earlier dramas, previous examples of comic interlude are rare, found only in *Elën*. Here the use of comic interlude is pronounced. The drinking scene between Moscone and Bob Upfill (150–60), for instance, is full of light moments. Vaudreuil's difficulty in retaining a clergyman to marry him is humorous (162), as is Tom Burnett's trouble with the tax officers (206–12) and with the Cherokee offering him a drink (215–16). Another example of comedy is when Bob Upfill, seeing the forest fire, asks whether his allies are going "to let us be grilled like rats" (295). Not unlike the comic moments in Shakespeare, the comedy here, furnished by the secondary characters, not only affords relief from the serious conflict of the main protagonists but by contrast adds poignancy to it.

From the foregoing discussion, it seems safe to conclude that Villiers intended *Le Nouveau Monde* to be a kind of *Gesamtkunstwerk*, a union of all arts, in vague imitation of Wagner's operas.[30] Not only do his extensive use of music and evident adaptation of the Wagnerian system of motifs suggest this, but so does his blending of psychological drama with the symbolic. Not only does the mixture of comedy with the ironic and serious hint at this, but so does his use of pictorial tableaux in combination with music and drama. The theory becomes all the more convincing when one remembers that *Le Nouveau Monde* was Villiers' first long play written after his trips to Germany. Now, the play may not be a masterpiece "written by a master of the stage":[31] The transition between Acts I and II is clumsy;[32] the drama slips at times into melodrama;[33] the action too often depends on coincidence.[34] Nonetheless, the play is a dazzling piece of theater that evinces both the playwright's determination to reform theater in France and his ever-developing knowledge of dramatic art.

Our analysis of Villiers' plays has been long and needs to be put in

perspective. Anxious to succeed as a playwright, Villiers successively wrote diverse types of theater, from the moralistic *L'Evasion*
to the historical *Le Prétendant* and the symbolic *Le Nouveau
Monde*. He was, however, little encouraged to produce *L'Evasion*,
and try as he might, prevailing tastes, unreceptive to his deep-seated
idealism, made it impossible for him to stage the two later works.
Nevertheless, these plays show marked improvement over his earlier ones, and *Le Nouveau Monde* indicates that Villiers was turning
away from dramas with a realistic framework to those with a symbolic foundation.

III   *Short Stories of the 1870s*

Between 1871 and 1879, Villiers published seventeen new short
stories, and in order to earn additional money as well as to attract
the public's attention, he also reprinted some earlier stories during
this period, sometimes with slight modification. Nine of the new
tales, in fact, saw two or more publications prior to 1880. For convenience sake, these stories can be grouped into four classes: satiric
tales, tales of mystery provoking terror and suspense, poetic tales
set in an earlier historic period, and a few stories that defy easy
classification.

A. *Satiric Stories*

The purpose of these works, as of satire in general, is to poke fun,
criticize, rebuke, but in a comic fashion: If Villiers wants to evoke
the reader's contempt for a subject, he also wants to amuse him.[35]
The eight satiric stories can be subdivided by form into two groups.
Four are narratives, with plot and characters, from which the author
is virtually absent. The other four are monologues. Speaking in his
own person or behind a thinly disguised mask, Villiers addresses
the reader directly.[36] Let us look first at the satiric monologues.

In "La Découverte de M. Grave" (1873, 1876), later titled
"L'Affichage céleste," Villiers lavishes praise on an idea "to turn the
firmament up to now unproductive to account" (*CC*, 52) and to
project, by means of "powerful streams of magnesium or electric
light," advertising slogans upon it (53). After enumerating the
benefits of the idea, the author expresses the wish that the inventor,
"supported by the cooperation of an enlightened government, begin
his important experiments" (57). In "La Machine à gloire" (1874),
Villiers lauds an invention by one Baron Bottom that "manufactures

glory" (*CC*, 61). After a discussion, supposedly conducted in rigorous scientific fashion, of glory and then of the claque (paid clappers
in the theater), the author claims Bottom's apparatus is "to the
Claque what the railroad is to the stagecoach" (71). No longer will
the claque or criticism be necessary. The machine, the "theater
itself" (72), provided with electrically run bellows producing sounds
of approval or disapproval, will influence the audience's reaction.
The success (or failure) of the play and the glory (or disgrace) of an
author will thus be ensured. Past glory for the author is even possible, since "the Machine can obtain retroactive results" (79). The
work ends by proclaiming that "modern dramatic Glory—such as
people of simple common sense conceive it— . . . is, now, WITHIN
THEIR REACH" (80).

"L'Appareil pour l'analyse chimique du dernier soupir" (1874,
1878) is a panegyric of a new device designed to ensure "the joy of
children and the tranquillity of parents," in short, "physical well-
being above all" (*CC*, 181). The use of the machine "vaccinates
against" suffering (184). No longer will children lose "time—time
that is money!—in useless flux of the lachrymal glands" when parents die (184); no longer will people be emotionally affected by art.
In his conclusion, the author admits that "the mixture contained in
the ball of multicolored crystal that constitutes the Device's form" is
derived from an explosive, but ironically adds that "nothing is more
inoffensive" (187). Finally, in "Le Traitement du Dr Tristan Chavassus" (1877), after giving a summary of recent discoveries, including
those of Grave and Bottom (*CC*, 265), Villiers extols a new one: a
treatment for "*Noises, Buzzings*, and all other troubles of the auditory canal" (265). By first sounding the word "Reality" ("Humanity"
in the 1883 edition) in one ear and variations of meaningless words
like "generosity" and "faith" in the other, then passing an electric
current through both, Chavassus can cure the patient of "buzzings
of glory, honor, and courage" (268). One leaves his office, a "man of
Humanity," "freed from all those useless *Voices*," feeling "Common
sense running, like a balm, through all your being" (269).

These stories resemble each other not only by their monologue
form but also by subject matter and satiric technique.[37] The primary
object of derision in the four tales is the same: modern science and
the blind faith the nineteenth century has in it as the panacea of
every human problem, every human woe. Science can illuminate a
dark sky; it can, with equal ease, ensure success to a drama and

happiness to humans. In none of these works, however, does the
satire stop there. Other attitudes of the century also incur the
satirist's displeasure. He derides the importance his contemporaries
place on utility and money (to the point of using the sky as a giant
billboard), their cult of common sense, and their insensitivity to true
human values like sentiment, art, and morality.

In all four works, Villiers constructs his satire in the same fashion.
He first reduces the stature of science by distorting its inventions
and exaggerating its pretensions *ad absurdum*. It is true that science
made boastful claims, but Villiers goes beyond these; he has it claim
to create a successful play and to vaccinate against despair. The
glory machine and Tristan's treatment do not realistically represent
the wonders of modern science; they caricaturize and ape them.[38]
Instead of ridiculing these outrageous claims and crazy inventions,
as we might expect, Villiers then does the opposite: Assuming the
posture of a science enthusiast, he treats them seriously and praises
them lavishly. "It concerns," he says in referring to the glory
machine, "a piece of news without equal in the recent annals of
Humanity" (*CC*, 61). Thanks to Grave's discovery, he writes, "the
Sky will finally be good for something and acquire an intrinsic value"
(58). The result is burlesque: an incongruous treatment of a ludicrous subject in a serious manner.[39] The reader laughs, not only
because the exaggeration and distortions in themselves are ridiculous, but also because of the incongruity between the subject and its
grand portrayal. In spite of his laughter, however, the reader is
jolted into seeing the painful truth in the satirist's exaggeration:
Contemporaries are heaping encomiums on something that perhaps
is not quite worth the attention and whose claims may be downright
silly.

The first of Villiers' satires in narrative form is "Les Demoiselles
de Bienfilâtre" (1874, 1875, 1876). In the preamble (*CC*, 3–4), the
narrator asserts "a certain human act is called crime, here, a good
action, over there, and reciprocally" (3). The rest of the story, divided into four parts, comically illustrates this moral relativity. In
the first part (5–6), the narrator sets the stage, describing first a café,
then its mundane life, finally the mundane women, "waiting [there]
for someone" (6). Among them are Olympe and Henriette de
Bienfilâtre. The second part sketches their background (6–8). Since
their parents were poor concierges, the girls became prostitutes,
"workers 'who go in day dress at night' " (7). They conducted their

"business" in such a fashion that they could with reason "carry their heads high" (8): They owed nothing to anyone, they honored all commitments, they put money aside for rainy days and retirement, they "closed on Sundays," and they paid no attention to young men's words "that only distract girls from the straight and narrow path of duty and work" (8). The third part, beginning with "One day, the younger [sister], Olympe, went bad" (8), describes a turn of events that upsets the equilibrium of their lives and introduces an element of tension into the story. Olympe has sinned by falling in love with Maxime, a student "poor like Job" (9), and has been neglecting her work. In the last part, the resolution of the story (10–14), Henriette makes a final effort to correct Olympe's wayward behavior by rebuking her love for a man "who does not [even] give her a radish" (11). Olympe's conscience is troubled, and she falls sick from shame. Feeling death near, fearing God's judgment, and wanting to gain absolution, she confesses to a priest. She has been guilty of having a "lover! For pleasure! Without gaining anything" (12). At the moment of absolution, Maxime enters, his hand full of money. A celestial smile lights Olympe's face. Taking Maxime's miraculous conversion to the bourgeois ethic as a sign, she dies, believing herself pardoned for her past sin.

In an attempt to poke fun, Villiers distorts and caricaturizes the materialistic society around him. Although the café setting is portrayed realistically (5), the morality and motivations of the characters are clearly exaggerations of morality and motives present in nineteenth century society. It may have been one's duty to earn money, but the complete inversion of what is ordinarily considered good and bad, whereby gainful prostitution is lauded and spontaneous emotion is faulted, is caricature. The reader laughs at the exaggeration, but at the same time the exaggeration makes him painfully aware of a truth: Money seems to be more highly prized than love.

The whole thing becomes more humorous since Villiers treats the exaggerated situation, involving characters of such little merit, with more dignity than it deserves. He raises the lowly to an elevated station by his serious, grandiose style. A theater near the café, for instance, recalls a "pagan temple" (5). The two prostitutes, Olympe and Henriette, come to the café at twilight, sitting down "in a well-lighted anfractuosity" (6). The lowly occupation of the girls' parents consists in "hanging on, at each moment, with despairing attitudes, to the long cord that corresponds to the lock of a carriage gateway" (6–7). At death's door, the common Olympe is described as closing "her eyelids as if to collect herself before opening her wings toward the infinite blue" (14). Twice Henriette's actions are accorded the nobility of the acts of heroes of yore. In the face of her sister's infidelity, she is described as smiling "like the young Spartan whose chest a fox was gnawing" (10). "Like Mallonia dishonored by Tiberius and going in front of the Roman Senate to accuse her ravisher before stabbing herself in her despair," Villiers says, she went to plead her case with Olympe (10–11). In addition, the preamble, with its serious exposition of moral relativity and the epigraph, "De la lumière," the supposed final statement of the great German philosopher Goethe, attribute to the story a grandeur and importance that its contents in fact do not have.

The situation is made still more funny by Villiers' use of irony, the device of saying the opposite of what one intends. For instance, the narrator calls the girls' education one of "good principles" (7) but means quite the contrary. He facetiously calls the sisters "exemplary" (8) and later Henriette "noble" (9). He terms Maxime "splendid" (13) precisely when it is evident that the young man, too, has been corrupted by the bourgeois ethic. Moreover, he describes Olympe as seeing herself "redeemed" or "bought back" by Maxime's actions (14), but he knows she has not only been lost to the bourgeois code but has also managed to corrupt her heretofore innocent lover. Finally, he has Olympe say that Maxime "has awakened to the light" of her code (14), but the narrator and audience realize that in bringing the money he has in truth capitulated to darkness and dullness. Olympe's words are all the more ironic since they call to mind Goethe's "De la lumière," used as the tale's epigraph; to her the words mean the converse of what Goethe's meant to him.

In "Le Plus Beau Dîner du monde" (1874), after a preamble sketching wagers won by ruses (CC, 158), the narrator relates in detail another example. Maître Percenoix proposes to stage the finest dinner in the world for the prominent townspeople of D***, where he has been practicing law for more than thirty years. He has long been in competition with his older colleague, Maître Lecastelier, and this dinner is to be the "battle ground . . . to finally have it out" (159). After much speculation in town about Percenoix's menu, the great day finally arrives. The townspeople line the street. The guests march in. The meal begins. Each guest must admit it is the finest dinner in the world. Taking up the challenge, however, Maître Lecastelier announces he will give "*a* finer one next year" (162). The year passes and the great day arrives. The townspeople again line the street. The guests march into Lecastelier's house. The meal begins. The dinner is the same as the one served by Percenoix the previous year, except for the twenty franc piece that each guest finds folded in his napkin. Lecastelier wins the wager, for it is agreed that his dinner is "the same . . . and nevertheless, it is finer!" No one can, however, put his finger "on the precise point that justified this undefinable impression of *difference*" between the meals (166).

In this story, Villiers pokes fun at the influence of money in modern bourgeois society and the accompanying intellectual dullness of its members. To make his reader laugh at the designated victims, Villiers uses techniques similar to those employed in "Les Demoiselles de Bienfilâtre." The first is caricature. The bourgeois may indeed by overly concerned with money and little concerned with self-examination, but Villiers exaggerates these qualities. His characters are so mesmerized by money that their judgment is easily manipulated by a twenty franc piece, and they are so intellectually blind that they are unable to perceive the obvious reason why they judged Lecastelier's dinner superior. A second technique Villiers uses is the portentously solemn style. The introduction, with its classical allusions, the grandiose turns of expression—"the angel of Emphyteosis" (159); "it was an undeclared war from the remotest of ages" (159); "Having arrived before the doorway, and at the sight of the signs [*panonceaux*] that glistened from the fires of the sunset, the guests turned around toward the magical horizon: the distant trees were lighted up; the birds quieted down in the near-by orchards" (160–61); "It was serious, very serious: the honor of the place was at stake" (163); "Mme Lecastelier did him the graciousness of blushing" (165)—as well as the scientific vocabulary at the end—"One comes well *within a hair,* as with the help of a 168th decimal, then the x of the statement draws back indefinitely, between those two assertions that confuse the human mind" (166)— are in sharp contrast with the banal subject of the story. They accord a dignity to the undistinguished lawyers that they do not have. This contrast between subject and style makes us laugh. A third technique Villiers uses in the tale to make us laugh is irony. For example, the narrator calls the supposed introducer of phylloxera (plant lice) in France "a celebrity" (160) but hardly means it. Moreover, he labels Percenoix's dinner "simple" (161), but then lists an extensive menu.

In "Le Secret de l'ancienne musique," published in 1878 over Villiers' protests as "Le Chapeau chinois" (*Corr*, I, 239–46), the orchestra of the Paris Opera is to study a work of a "certain German composer (whose name, already forgotten, happily eludes us)" (*CC*, 141). On seeing the piece, the conductor calls it unexecutable since it requires a Chinese pavilion, a military instrument fallen into disuse in France. As luck would have it, the cymbal player knows an old professor of the Chinese pavilion, a "representative of the old Music" (145), who agrees to play the needed part for the orchestra. It is soon evident that the composer has placed "with a German harshness, a rancorous malignity . . . almost insurmountable difficulties" in that part: it consists "exclusively of silences" (146). At first, the old artist plays with such mastery that it seems he can sometimes be heard. Then, he gives up. "It is too difficult . . . , " he shouts, "There is no melody there. It is charivari! Art is lost!" (147). In the original version, he is overcome with anger and falls dead into a bass drum, taking away with him "the secret of the charms of the old music" (452).[40]

Clearly, Villiers is ridiculing the conservative taste, closed-mindedness, and avowed hostility toward Wagner (a "certain German composer") prevalent in French musical circles in the 1860s and 1870s. Here too he draws his adversaries in caricatural terms. Not only does the orchestra director "shudder" at the sight of the score (142), but the orchestra is plunged into "that state the physiologists call the *comatose* state" (143) and the old professor, invoking "My country above all" (145), consents to play the Chinese pavilion out of a sense of patriotic duty. Sometimes Villiers makes us laugh by ennobling the ludicrous events with grandiose description. The men who consult the old musician, for example, are described as "ambassadors" entering his "sanctuary" (144), and at the professor's entrance to the Opera the following morning, "everyone stood up, paying him homage like a kind of posterity" (145). Other times, he provokes our laughter by debasing the characters. His depersonification of orchestra members by equating them with their instruments—"The cymbals appeared like a savior! The conductor kissed [him] . . . . The trombones, touched, encouraged him with their smiles; a countrabass gave him an envious glance . . . "

(143)—calls to mind a fable; and the story's ending, with the professor falling into the bass drum, borders on slapstick. Additionally, Villiers provokes laughter through irony. One such example is the narrator's "happily" forgetting Wagner's name (141); another is calling the German composer "the presumptuous innovator" (142). Dubbing the old musician "an illustrious professor" (452) is also meant ironically.

The last of the satiric tales is "Virginie et Paul" (1874, 1875, 1876), composed of three parts. In the introduction (*CC*, 91–93), the narrator, who has by chance arrived before the gate of a girls' school, formerly an old monastery, reminisces about a blissful romance he had as a youth. His narration is interrupted by the rendezvous of young lovers after whom the tale is named and a dialogue that forms the body of the story (93–95). Paul gives Virginie a bouquet that didn't "cost any money" (93). Paul stayed late with his father "so that he would give [him] a little money" (93). Paul is to become a lawyer and gain a little money. Virginie is happier in the girls' school now that the headmistress "can spend a little more money" (94). A relative is old and will leave them a little money. Virginie's mother will give her, as a dowry, a small house in the country that will "also bring in a little money" (95). One can live more economically in the country than in town. Fearful that the headmistress of the school will be awakened and that Paul's father will notice his son's absence, the lovers part. Dialogue ceases, and in the conclusion (95–96), the passer-by resumes his narration. The lovers' words, "evoking other *almost* similar memories . . . make [him]," he confesses, "shed soft tears" (96).

As in "Les Demoiselles de Bienfilâtre," in this tale Villiers satirizes the modern world's concern for money and its subjection of love to financial calculation. Here, however, Villiers uses more dialogue than he does in "Les Demoiselles," and the satire results primarily from the contrast he develops between the tale's beginning and the dialogue of the lovers. The story's title, alluding to Bernardin de Saint-Pierre's idyllic *Paul et Virginie* (1787), the Latin epigraph "In the friendly silence of the moon" taken from Vergil's *Ecologues* (42–39 B.C.), and the poetic style of the passer-by's narration all suggest an idyll, a blissful state of perfect love. But, as the passer-by intimates in noting that the school was formerly a monastery, times have changed. The reader's expectations are dashed by the discordant words of modern-day lovers, whose union is more a financial consideration than a sentimental one. The word "argent," which the passer-by used poetically in the sense of "silver" (91, 93), takes on the prosaic sense of "money" in the couple's speech. The word echoes and reechoes throughout the dialogue. Their obsession with money is so great and the word "argent" is so present in their psyche that they can only characterize the nightingale's voice and the moon by derivative forms of that word: "argentine," "argentée" (94). Villiers' intent to satirize the depoetization of love in the modern world becomes still clearer with the passer-by's final words. While it is evident from the introduction that his romantic experience has been vastly different from Virginie and Paul's, the narrator contents himself with saying in ironic fashion that they were *"almost* similar." Likewise, his statement that the crass scene he has just witnessed "make[s] [him] shed soft tears" can only be taken ironically.

B. *Tales of Mystery and Suspense*

The first of Villiers' tales of mystery and suspense is "Véra" (1874, 1876), set in Paris in these "recent years" (*CC*, 15). Count d'Athol returns home one autumn night, after burying his beloved wife Véra and throwing the silver mausoleum key within the tomb so as "not to come back any more" (17). He thinks of their past together: their meeting, their personalities ("Certain ideas, that of the soul, for example, of Infinity, *even of God*, were as if veiled from their understanding" [18]), their perfect union isolated from the world. He summons a servant to announce that the countess and he will dine at ten o'clock and that *they* will receive no one in the future. Henceforth, with the servant's cooperation, D'Athol lives beside an illusion, in absolute "ignorance of his beloved's death" (21). A year later, on the very anniversary of her death, D'Athol senses the presence of his wife: warmth in her jewels, blood on a handkerchief, a turned page on the piano, fresh flowers in the room. The clock, silent for a year, now sounds the hour. Véra has been called forth by the count's unswerving faith in her existence. The two kiss and fuse into "a single being" (26). Suddenly, D'Athol remembers that his wife has died. All signs of her presence vanish at that very instant. The count sorrowfully asks how he can again reach his departed beloved. As a response, the silver mausoleum key falls from the marriage bed, and a ray of light illuminates it.

Villiers' intent in this tale is similar to that in "Claire Lenoir" and

"L'Intersigne." In all three, Villiers seeks to disorient the reader and to compel him, like the sceptical protagonist, into contemplating the possibility of a mysterious beyond. But despite its suspense, luxuriant prose, and subtle delineation of character, there is a problem with "Véra." Perhaps more than "Claire" or "L'Intersigne," this story is based on abstract philosophical theories. Unless one understands these theories, the story does not make much sense and one is not motivated to contemplate the beyond. Castex was right to state that the tale's "philosophical abstraction spoils a bit the desired effect."[41]

It is true that the original 1874 version, ending with the lovers' embrace (26), was not too difficult to understand. D'Athol performs prescribed rites (suggested by Eliphas Lévi) and thereby resurrects the shade of his dead wife. Less comprehensible is the 1876 version, expanded and modified to give it a reading less illustrative of occultism than of illusionistic philosophy.[42] Here, Véra is present solely because D'Athol believes her to be. As soon as his faith waivers and he exclaims: "But you have died!" (26), the illusion is broken and evidence of her presence vanishes. If that is the proper sense of the 1876 version, what then is the meaning of the silver key that falls from the marriage bed? In all probability, Villiers meant to show two things: first, that the illusion created by the will does have an objective reality,[43] since Véra herself must have brought the key from the mausoleum to the mansion; and second, that D'Anthol and Véra's love can only be resumed in death, since Vera indicates the key to her tomb as the way the count can join her. The idea of afterlife, however, is foreign to illusionistic philosophy, on which the other elements of the second version are based.[44]

In "L'Inconnue" (1876, 1879), Count Félicien de la Vierge has arrived in Paris that very morning from Brittany. At the farewell performance of soprano Maria-Felicia Malibran (1808–1836), he spies a beautiful, mysterious unknown woman; after the performance, he follows her. She tells him she is deaf, but this loss has permitted her to develop an interior sense, liberating her from "that intellectual deafness of which most other women are the victims" (*CC*, 248). She can read other people's feelings and predict "the value and quality of these feelings" (248); her soul is "sensitive to the vibrations of eternal things" (248). She refuses Félicien's offer of love, for love, like everything here below except thought, "is only an ILLUSION" (251). The story ends with the stranger's departing "like a bird" and the count's returning to his solitary Breton castle "never to be heard of again" (253).

The stranger's deafness, like Claire Lenoir's blindness and Tullia Fabriana's isolation from the material world, suggests and explains her almost superhuman understanding of realities that elude the senses. She perceives, for one thing, the emptiness of human discourse in which the same meaningless words are repeated over and over again. For another, she realizes, much like Tullia in *Isis* (*OC*, *IX*, 214–15), that love of another may be impossible: Man can love only that which he can know. Since knowledge is subjective, he can only know his perception of people and reality, not the people and reality themselves.[45]

Much has already been written about these ideas. Not enough has been said about the dramatic role they play or the sense of mystery that pervades the tale. Félicien de la Vierge is obviously one of those sensitive people, destined to live apart from the world with knowledge of eternal things. Not only does his name suggest this purity, but so do his place of origin, the château Blanchelande (Whiteheath), and the "unknown sign" the deaf woman sees on his forehead (248). He has, however, been distracted by a "curiosity of our wonderful hell," Paris (240). Although one does not fully understand how, Félicien and the stranger have been destined for one another (241), but not in the way Félicien at first thinks. She is not to be his mistress, but a revealer of "a world that unveils itself" (241). By her revelations about life and love, she frightens Félicien (252) into returning to his castle and his destiny. The comparison of the deaf woman to a bird (253) is not at all fortuitous. It recalls that she is like the swan of the story's epigraph that "is silent all its life to sing well only once" (239). Her performance completed, like the swan, she disappears (253). This final performance of the deaf woman is foreshadowed by Malibran's farewell operatic appearance, mentioned at the beginning of the story.

Like "L'Inconnue," "Le Convive inconnu" (1874), later titled "Le Convive des dernières fêtes," is about a mysterious person who has a critical effect upon the other character(s) in the story. During the carnival of 186–, the narrator and his friend C*** invite three beautiful acquaintances, Clio la Cendrée, Antonie Chantilly, and Annah Jackson, to dine with them. They are joined by a certain Baron Von H***, whom the narrator once met in Wiesbaden and who presents himself as Baron Saturn. The narrator later remembers also having seen the stranger in the south near a guillotine. He takes him to be the executioner come to town to perform a decapitation the following morning. After the stranger leaves, Dr. Florian Les Eglisottes enters the restaurant and fully unmasks the rich baron. Cruel instincts were awakened in him during a trip to the Orient. His inability to be named "head torturer of the world" has maddened him further (*CC*, 123, 125). He now goes from execution to execution, often bribing the headman "to let him operate" (123). These revelations not only make C*** "shudder from an indefinable horror" (125) but also make Clio la Cendrée "feel indisposed" (126) and drive Antonie to sell her blood-colored stone for the benefit of the poor.

Before plummeting characters and reader alike into a horrible awareness, Villiers does a masterful job of creating suspense about the stranger's identity. The baron's "eastern paleness" (99) and his assumed name, Saturn, betokening a cursed sign (100), put the reader on guard, as does mention of his early morning meeting (101). The fact that the narrator and C*** shudder at his manner of emphasizing words (105) makes one more uneasy. The suspense is heightened still further by the narrator's recollection of seeing Saturn somewhere besides Wiesbaden (105) and by his inability to recall the precise circumstances. Further mention of the morning meeting (112), as well as the baron's statement that "I am blind and deaf as often as God permits" (113), causes the characters and reader to speculate further about his identity. Puns like "kill time" (101) and "Are you losing your head?" (117) conjure up ominous notions and contribute to the suspense. Even when the narrator remembers that he has seen Saturn near a guillotine and assumes that he is the visiting executioner, C***'s remark that his friend is "seeing executioners everywhere" (118) casts the reader once again into doubt and renews the suspense. Only the doctor's horrible revelation dispels the mystery.

C. *Poetic Tales*

We turn now to two tales that in form closely resemble prose poems. The first of these is "Souvenirs occultes" (1878), which is, in fact, a reworking of Villiers' early prose poem entitled "El Desdichado." Many lines from the poem have been retained in the tale. A long description of the dead cities (*CC*, 278–80), however, has been interpolated into the new version, and the narration of the adventurer's nocturnal escapades and eventual betrayal (280–82) has been greatly amplified. [46]

The second tale is "Impatience de la foule" (1876, 1879), which consists of four parts. The introduction (*CC*, 132–34) contains a description of setting—ancient Sparta during the first days of winter—and a flashback that recalls events beginning two days earlier. After the Lacedaemonian Three Hundred's departure for battle, it was reported that a shepherd had revealed to the Persians a pass in the region of Phocis and that the enemy was now invading Greece. The senate gave orders to defend the city. The second part (134–36) returns to the present. The Spartan citizens, upon the ramparts, await the approaching Persian army. Some think they see far off the reflection of Xerxes' cavalry. The priests claim to hear noise coming from the north. The veterans calculate the number of Persians they will kill before they themselves fall. A flock of ravens then alights on the sacred woods, and the maidens begin to worry, wondering why the holy suicidal swords have been distributed. A man is sighted in the distance, and part three (136–39) describes his approach toward the city. Thinking that he is fleeing a victorious enemy and that the defeated Spartan troops will soon follow, the angry citizens hurl insults at the warrior, his fiancée throws a rock at him, and the cook spits upon him. In the last part (139–40), Villiers describes the death of the warrior, shut out of the city by the vengeful crowd and ravaged by the vigilant ravens. The supposed deserter is in truth "the messenger of Victory elected by the Three Hundred" (140).

It is apparent that in composing this tale, Villiers relied on two known legends. One, reported by Herodotus, is about the Spartan deserter who suffered harsh treatment at the hands of his fellow citizens; the other concerns the warrior who fell dead from exhaustion after carrying news of victory at Marathon to Athens. [47] Villiers, however, mixes the two and presents an ironic situation whereby the supposedly defeated Greek army is victorious and the heroic runner is mistaken for a coward. This ironic twist at the tale's conclusion is a complete surprise for two reasons. First, until the end, the author focuses attention on the Spartan citizens; the reader's knowledge is limited to their opinions. Consequently, as their imaginations are fed by reports of invasion and the arrival of ravens, and as they fantasize about their army's defeat, the reader likewise comes to believe that the Spartans have been decimated. To the reader, the runner can only be fleeing the advancing Persian army. Second, the preponderance of death imagery—the setting winter sun (132), the suggestion of slaughter (132), the vigilant and rapacious ravens (135–36)—suggests a calamity of major proportions, such as the defeat and destruction of the Spartan army, not simply the death of a solitary runner.

In addition to the tale's structure, unexpected conclusion, and images, mention should also be made of its musiclike prose. This musicality derives, first of all, from the rhythm of the long descriptive sentences, subdivided into phrases, that flow with utter grace one into another. Second, Villiers makes extensive use of alliteration. For instance, he wrote: "La poudreuse pente du mont rougeoyait des feux froids . . ." (132); "Soudain, l'une d'elles s'approcha, svelte et pâle, du rempart" (138); and "Une sorte de colère sacrée lui fit oublier ses devoirs" (139).[48] Finally, the prose's musical quality owes much to the use of onomatopoeia. The predominance of sibilant sounds in "Cependant, cette multitude aux bouches sévères se condamnait au silence à cause des vierges" (134),[49] actually suggests the silence the crowd imposes on itself. Another example is the sentence, "Les catapultes ronflèrent, envoyant des volées de cailloux dont les chocs sonnèrent après mille sifflements . . ." (136).[50] Here the double *r* of "ronflèrent" evokes the sound of catapults in motion, while the *sfl* combination of "sifflements" suggests a whizz and the harsh consonants in "chocs," the impact of stone.

D. *Miscellaneous Tales*

Of the remaining tales, "A s'y méprendre" (1875)—the story of a man who takes refuge from a November drizzle in the Paris morgue, goes to a café for a business meeting, sees (or thinks he sees) the same things he saw in the morgue, and finally returns home, resolving *"never [again] to do business"* (*CC*, 131)—displays characteristics of both the satiric and the suspense story. The satiric intention is clear. By using the same words to describe the morgue and the businessman's haunt (129, 131), Villiers suggests that the world of business is a kind of life-in-death. Not only does the businessman work in a deadly atmosphere but he himself is lifeless, without color, and without thought. In spite of the satiric intent, the evocation of death, eerie details ("an apparition of stone," "dismal and fantastic vapor" [129]), the hallucination, and the narrator's terrified reaction create a tone that closely resembles that of Villiers' tales of suspense.

Two tales, "Le Médaillon" (1874, 1875, later called "Antonie") and "Sentimentalisme" (1876), are psychological studies, mixed with satire. In the former story, the description of Antonie turning "toward us, with airs of Cleopatra, . . . to see *herself* again [reflected] in our eyes" (*CC*, 59) suggests a vanity inharmonious with the romantic setting of violets, wine, and candlelight. The courtesan's self-centeredness becomes blatantly obvious when she admits carrying in her medaillon, not a lover's lock, but one of her own, "*in a spirit of loyalty*" (60).

In "Sentimentalisme," Lucienne Emery accuses artists, and in particular Count Maximilien de W***, with whom her "intimacy hardly dated six months" (*CC*, 149), of blunting "the faculty of *really* undergoing the torments or pleasures Fate allots to them" (149). Maximilien attempts to answer these charges, but is interrupted by his mistress, who asks the time. She is breaking off their liaison; in an hour and a half, she is meeting another man. Maximilien hides his true feelings. At Lucienne's insistence, he continues his analysis. The quality of feeling is different in artists. In them sensations, once felt, develop, while in ordinary people they are soon forgotten. Having attained "a purity of sensations inaccessible to the profane," artists would be liars if they "borrowed . . . accepted pantomimes and . . . 'consecrated' expressions" to translate their own feelings (154). As a result, Maximilien concludes, people wrongly consider artists hard of heart. Lucienne is little persuaded by this argument. All she knows is that Maximilien "eludes" her and she must leave him (155). Returning home, Maximilian shoots himself fatally in the chest. Henceforth, when asked why she wears black, Lucienne answers that it suits her so well. Her mourning fan "then flutters over her breast like a moth's wing over a tombstone" (157).

The principal interest of this tale lies in the contrast Villiers develops between Lucienne Emery, epitomizing "ordinary" people (155) with their "accepted pantomimes and . . . 'consecrated' expressions" (154), and Maximilien, who typifies the artist. Although Lucienne accuses Maximilien of being insensitive, he is, as he tries to demonstrate in his analysis of the artistic temperament, more sensitive than ordinary men. His dramatic suicide over the breakup with Lucienne attests to this depth of feeling. In truth, it is not the noble artist who is insensitive, but the bourgeois critic. Not only does Lucienne not understand her lover of six months, but she utterly disregards his feelings, abruptly announcing the end of their love and her imminent rendezvous with another man. Even after Maximilien's suicide, she hardly shows more feeling. Granted, she wears black and her fan nervously flutters when asked the reason for the dark attire. But, otherwise, her life is substantially unaffected. She answers new lovers "in a playful tone" (157). Her bosom is as ever "a tombstone" (157). True feeling in most people, as Maximilien pointed out, is so weak (150–51).

Finally, "Succès d'estime" (1877), later called "Sombre récit, conteur plus sombre," is about a dramatist D***, unable to distinguish life from theater, who serves as his friend's second in a duel. One of the most complex tales Villiers wrote between 1871 and 1879, it contains humor, satire, social commentary, suspense, character analysis, and autobiography (most characters being based on playwrights whose facile successes Villiers detested). What is more, it is a tale within a tale; a narrator relates the story he heard D*** tell at a dinner party. Even though the narrator contends that he is "leaving the words strictly" to D*** (*CC*, 208), he constantly interrupts the narration (210, 211, 212, 213, 215, 216, 217) to indicate the speaker's expressions and gestures, the other listeners' reactions, and his own. As Gourevitch intimates, the point of view from which this tale is told, with a double perspective of speaker and narrator, is as important to its success as the intriguing plot.[51]

Four conclusions can be drawn from our discussion of the short stories. First, the tales display great variety in tone, structure, theme, and narrative perspective. Even so, Villiers shows a marked preference for the satiric tale (perhaps reflecting the bitterness he experienced in these years), and the theme of an ideal world figures in many of the rest. Second, it is apparent that Edgar Allan Poe exercised an enduring influence on Villiers' writing. This influence is discernible not only in the suspenseful "Véra" but also in "Le Convive," where the character Saturn suffers from a morbid, pathological condition. A trace of Poe's "Unparalleled Adventure of One Hans Pfaall" and "The Balloon-Hoax" may also be evident in such pseudoscientific tales as "L'Appareil pour l'analyse chimique du dernier soupir." On the other hand, the influence of Hegelianism, apparent in works of the 1860s and early 1870s, was not as long-lasting. The tales show little influence of the German philosopher, and Villiers must have realized that much more separated him from Hegel than actually united him.[52] Moreover, as the revisions of "Véra" show and as "L'Inconnue" confirms, Villiers was moving away from occult doctrines to an illusionism derived from German idealism.[53] Third, not only "Succès d'estime," but many of the other tales, are heavily autobiographical. "Souvenirs occultes" is about his ancestor Jean-Jérôme. Félicien de la Vierge's familial history recalls Villiers; the narrator's idyllic love in "Virginie et Paul" is not unlike his own as an adolescent. Baron Saturn's obsession with executions is evidently one Villiers himself shared (*Corr*, II, 87). And Maximilien of "Sentimentalisme," an artist misunderstood by women and society, is a self-portrait, just as Félicien of "L'Inconnue" surely is. Finally, despite the philosophical abstraction and inconsistencies in "Véra," the stories as a group maintain the high quality set by Villiers' earlier three. In fact, at least in one area, there is noticeable improvement. Most of the satiric tales maintain a unity of tone and mood that was sorely lacking in "Claire Lenoir."

CHAPTER 4

Moments of Triumph

I Family Life, Growing Celebrity, Painful
Death (1880–1889)

ALTHOUGH in 1879 Villiers was better known for his personal-ity than for his writing, this situation was soon to change, as the author's publication gradually increased after 1880. Changes in Villiers' personal life had much to do with this rise in publication. Around 1880 Villiers became involved with Marie Dantine, a sim-ple, barely literate widow, who had cared for him when he was ill with pneumonia.[1] She had a boy, Albert, from her first marriage, and in 1881 she bore Villiers a son, Victor, known to all as Totor. Marie and the children were undoubtedly a great solace to Villiers' lonely existence. Nevertheless, they placed upon him the additional responsibility of sustaining three other lives. Furthermore, the death of Villiers' mother on 12 April 1882 (*Corr*, II, 16–18) left the author totally responsible for his semisenile and partially paralyzed father. In the face of these new obligations, Villiers could no longer be as indifferent to his material situation as he once was; he was forced to seize every opportunity to earn money. The result was a dramatic rise in the number of his works, especially short stories. Increased literary production alone, however, cannot explain Vil-liers' increased publication. Changes of attitude in literary circles were also a contributing factor. Around 1880, the public was grow-ing tired of realistic-naturalistic works and more receptive to the idealistic philosophy Villiers had been preaching. Writers like Baudelaire, Mallarmé, Verlaine, and Rimbaud, heretofore ridi-culed, were now in vogue. Consequently, editors were more willing to read Villiers with sympathy and to give his work the outlet that had been previously denied.[2]

In 1880 alone, Villiers not only published *Le Nouveau Monde* and
three new tales ("Histoire d'amour du vieux temps" ["La Reine
Ysabeau"], "Vox populi," "Fleurs de ténèbres"), he also reprinted
four stories ("Les Demoiselles de Bienfilâtre," "Véra," "Virginie et
Paul" "Impatience de la foule") and began publishing a first version
of *L'Eve future* in serial form. The increasing number of publications
did much to attract attention, and his growing repute as an author is
suggested by the fact that he was asked to be the monarchist candidate for the municipal council of Paris from the seventeenth arrondissement (*Corr*, II, 10). In all likelihood, the monarchist faction
was counting heavily on Villiers' reputation as a writer (as well as his
aristocratic name) to defend its ideas in the press. His nascent
notoriety, however, did not carry the day. In the elections of 9
January 1881, Villiers lost soundly to Severiano de Heredia, former
president of the council and a leftist. The vote was 2147 to 633.[3]

Villiers' publications continued to grow after 1881. In 1881–1882,
he published two new stories ("Le Désir d'être un homme," "Les
Brigands") and reprinted five other ones ("Vox populi," "L'Affichage
céleste," "Le Plus Beau Dîner du monde," "L'Appareil pour
l'analyse chimique du dernier soupir," "Duel au pistolet" ["Sombre
récit, conteur plus sombre"]). Then, in rapid succession, three
events occurred that were to thrust his name before the public and
assure him a long-awaited celebrity.

On 9 February 1883, Villiers' short stories, under the title *Contes
cruels*, were published by Calmann-Lévy, ironically the very publisher who had rejected them six years earlier. Although the volume
was not a financial success, it was of utmost importance as it
gathered together Villiers' stories, previously scattered in out-of-
the-way papers, placed them in the public eye, and made the author's talents visible to everyone.[4] "These tales . . .," as Remy de
Gourmont expressed it, "finally put Villiers de l'Isle-Adam in his
[rightful] place."[5] A second important event occurred ten days later.
Le Nouveau Monde, which Villiers heretofore had little success in
staging, much to his resentment (*Corr*, I, 276–77, 281–82), finally
had its premiere on 19 February 1883 at the Théâtre des Nations.
For the opening, Villiers asked Henry Ghys, musician and composer, to write an overture (*Corr*, II, 23) to supplement the music
he himself had written (*Corr*, II, 27). It turned out, however, that
another friend, Alexandre Georges, composed this music (*Corr*, II,

27). Despite the great time and energy devoted to rehearsals (*Corr*, II, 28), the results were disappointing. Several actors decided to sabotage the performance by playing their parts in a ludicrous fashion. It is thought that Mlle Rousseil, who played Mistress Andrews, persuaded her colleagues, out of retaliation for being denied the more important role of Ruth Moore, to join her in disgracing the author (*Corr*, II, 29). In any event, the critics recognized that the play's failure was not Villiers' fault—"Let us have the courage," wrote one, "to declare it in all frankness, M. Villiers de l'Isle-Adam's work, notable in certain respects, suffered chiefly from faulty acting"[6]—and were not unkind in their criticism. The kind remarks of critics and the intrigue surrounding the premiere helped to publicize Villiers' name. A third event destined to increase his fame occurred in September 1884. This was the publication of Joris-Karl Huysmans' novel *A Rebours,* in which Villiers figured, along with Verlaine, Corbière, Aloysius Bertrand, Mallarmé, and Poe, among the protagonist's favorite writers. Des Esseintes' literary tastes were to have a great influence on the esthetic orientation of the younger generation, and Villiers' fame spread among the young as a result of this mention by Huysmans.

After suffering so much, Villiers must have marveled with a little disbelief at his celebrity. Despite growing fame, however, Villiers was not without difficulties. He had sold the rights to the *Contes cruels* for a meager 375 francs, an amount quickly depleted. The premiere of *Le Nouveau Monde* brought in little or nothing. True, it was now easier for him to have stories published—from April 1883 he collaborated regularly with *Le Figaro* and from August 1884 with *Le Gil Blas*—but the 100-odd francs he received for each acceptance were not always adequate to provide for four people (*Corr*, II, 50). Indeed, he sometimes did not have money to pay the rent and had to change lodgings. Moreover, the smallness of the quarters in which Villiers and his family were forced to live caused problems. In spite of the affection he felt for Albert and his love for Totor (whom he frequently took along to cafés or to visit friends), the din of children must have more than once irritated Villiers and interrupted his writing. He in fact once asked to use a friend's apartment so that he could work in quiet, away from the "shouting of my retinue" (*Corr*, II, 137).

Added to the difficulties within the household were those with the senile Joseph-Toussaint. Villiers' father would die on 1 December 1885, but in his last two years, 1884–1885, he made Villiers' existence very uncomfortable. Not only was he perpetually asking a none-too-rich Villiers for money (*Corr*, II, 77, 78, 84), he also plagued him with chimeric stories of marrying a rich woman (*Corr*, II, 69, 71, 72, 84) and promises of securing one for his son (*Corr*, II, 80). Worse than that, the eighty year old man unjustly blamed the beloved Aunt Kérinou for causing the family's ruin (*Corr*, II, 89); constantly reprimanded Villiers for rudeness to Louise (apparently some predatory companion of his [*Corr*, II, 57, 60, 66, 79]); and rebuked his son when he learned about the liaison with the common and illiterate Marie Dantine (*Corr*, II, 62). Luckily for Villiers, there were two new people in his life with whom he could share these problems. The first was Léon Bloy, whom he met at Nina de Villard's around 1878 but with whom he developed more intimate ties only after 1884 when the former's *Révélateur du globe* first appeared. The second was Huysmans, who became a close friend after the publication of *A Rebours* (1884) although they had known each other since 1876.

By 1885, Villiers' work was being sought by publishers (*Corr*, II, 83, 85, 98). Now free of the debilitating thought of having works unpublished, Villiers entered a period of still greater literary production. He collaborated with *La Vie moderne* to publish the definitive *L'Eve future* (13 June 1885–27 March 1886) and with *La Jeune France* to publish the first complete version of *Axël* (November 1885–June 1886). Between 1885 and 1886, *Le Figaro*, *Le Succès*, *Le Chat noir*, and *La Revue contemporaine* published seven stories, and on 25 March 1886 in the latter review appeared *L'Evasion*, a drama actually composed in 1871. Furthermore, in 1886, Villiers began a collaboration with Maurice de Brunhoff, who successively published in book form *L'Eve future* (4 May 1886), the long tale *Akëdysséril* (2 July 1886), and finally *L'Amour suprême* (24 July 1886), a collection that contained twelve tales, all written after 1883. With this amount of work, it is little wonder that Villiers should have no time (especially unremunerated time) to help an aspiring poet correct his verse (*Corr*, II, 112). It is no less a wonder that by the fall of 1886 he should be exhausted and that his bronchial condition should be severely aggravated. On 9 September 1886, therefore, Villiers wrote to Mallarmé, on vacation in Valvins par Avon (Seine-et-Marne), saying that he was "suffering, seriously this time, from a dilation of the bronchi, by dint of coughing," and asking his friend to "mail the address of Dr. Robin" (*Corr*, II, 135).

Despite the bronchitis and persistent illness (*Corr*, II, 160, 194, 195, 197), Villiers still managed to work feverishly. Prompted in all likelihood by the publicity Huysmans' *A Rebours* had given Bonhomet, protagonist of "Claire Lenoir," Villiers began writing additional tales about him. By May 1887 a collection appeared that included not only a slightly revised "Claire Lenoir" but also four other tales devoted to the now famous bourgeois doctor. It was called *Tribulat Bonhomet*. In autumn of the same year, Villiers was involved with the readings and rehearsals of his play *L'Evasion*, which Antoine, director at the Free Theater, had asked to stage (*Corr*, II, 178). The play's successful premiere on 11 October 1887 must have surprised and overjoyed Villiers, who had, after two theatrical failures, given up all hope of seeing a play of his acclaimed.[7] Finally, on 27 February of the following year, he published *Histoires insolites*, containing twenty tales, all of which, except three, had been published individually between 1883 and 1887, and the *Nouveaux Contes cruels*, a collection of stories published earlier that year in *La Vie pour rire*, *Le Gil Blas*, *Le Figaro*, and *La Revue libre*, appeared on 13 November 1888.

Villiers did interrupt his writing in 1888 long enough to take two trips. The first was to Belgium, where he had been negotiating since late 1886 to deliver a series of readings from his works (*Corr*, II, 148–49). The series, readings from *Histoires insolites*, was finally organized to coincide with a production of his *L'Evasion* that was to open in Brussels on 16 February 1888. Villiers left Paris on 13 February and attended the Belgian premiere. He was delighted not only by the enthusiastic reception of his play but also by the complimentary press notices of the readings that followed (*Corr*, II, 215–16, 220). He was less pleased, however, with the food, the accomodations, and the fact he was picking up the Belgian accent (*Corr*, II, 218, 225). But worse, he was totally distraught when he learned that he would be earning less from the trip than he had expected: "What good is renown and the fuss and the applause I have received here, and all the enthusiastic press of Belgium, when one does not have a little money to wait for!" (*Corr*, II, 221). He delivered talks in Brussels, Liège, and Ghent. But others were never held, it seems, "because of the cold weather" (*Corr*, II, 225). He stayed on, hoping new lectures would materialize (*Corr*, II,

228), but nothing did. At length, disappointed and homesick, with receipts of only six hundred francs, Villiers left for Paris on 10 March 1888. Léon Bloy, who in part financed the trip, mistakenly thought Villiers made a fortune. Unfortunately, this misconception would be the source of a falling out when Villiers later did not (and probably could not) come to his financial aid (*Corr*, II, 241–43).

Villiers' second trip was to Dieppe. Since September 1887, Bloy had been urging Villiers to visit Lord Cecil Marquis of Salisbury, who was on holiday in the Norman port, and solicit his financial support. After all, the rich British aristocrat might be willing to come to the aid of an impoverished French counterpart (*Corr*, II, 190–91), especially one who had sought his advice about *Le Nouveau Monde* and had even dedicated "L'Annonciateur" and *Akëdysséril* to him. Perhaps it was the financial disappointment of the Belgian tour that finally induced Villiers to take Bloy's advice to heart. In any event, in late September 1888, Villiers went to Dieppe, received Lord Salisbury at his hotel, but returned to Paris several days later, completely empty-handed. The British nobleman, it seems, was unresponsive to the Frenchman's needs (*Corr*, II, 244–45).

Shortly after his return, Villiers became seriously ill (*Corr*, II, 265). He had long suffered from bronchitis and stomach pains, but now he was dying, worn out by years of privation and persistent poverty. Although he probably never knew what was wrong, being told it was a dilation of the stomach that would subside, the malady was diagnosed by Dr. Albert Robin as stomach cancer.[8] When Mallarmé found out, he organized an appeal for monthly contributions to support the dying man and his family. Ironically, at a time when it seemed to matter little, Villiers' renown was never greater. He had only recently been asked to write a preface for a translation of Poe's verse (*Corr*, II, 207), his name was included in the 1888 edition of Verlaine's *Poètes maudits*, and his portrait had just appeared on the 15 January 1889 cover of *La Revue illustrée*.

On the advice of doctors, Villiers soon left his unhealthy quarters in Paris to go live in the country. It was not enough that his stomach hurt, he digested food with difficulty, and he suffered from diarrhea. By the worst stroke of luck, the house he rented in the country, in Nogent-sur-Marne, just east of the capital, turned out to be damp, and this dampness caused a recurrence of his bronchitis. In a letter to Mallarmé, Villiers relates how "shortness of breath prevent[ed]

[him] from taking three steps" and how he was forced to assume the position of "a consonant V" so he could breathe more easily (*Corr*, II, 288). As Villiers' condition became worse, Huysmans suggested that he try to gain admittance to the Maison de Santé des Frères Saint-Jean de Dieu in Paris. Villiers agreed and, through the poet François Coppée, he was able to get a room there. On 12 July 1889 Villiers was moved to the hospital in the seventh arrondissement.

Villiers' end was now near. Recognizing this fact, Mallarmé and Huysmans worried about Marie and Totor's future. Friends had supported them for five months, but this could not go on indefinitely. Aid would have to be sought from public sources. The difficulty was that Totor, registered at birth under his mother's name, was illegitimate in the eyes of the law, and an illegitimate child stood little chance of being granted support from the Ministry of Public Instruction. Villiers could legitimize Totor and guarantee him a stipend by marrying Marie. But this he was unwilling to do, at least not while there remained any hope of survival. Although he had lived with Marie nearly ten years, his aristocratic pride prevented him from even contemplating life with an illiterate, common Luxembourgeois wife. Villiers' attitude must have frustrated Huysmans, who knew that no chance of survival remained and that death might intervene at any moment. On 9 August, therefore, he enlisted the aid of Fr. Sylvestre, chaplain of the home, to persuade Villiers to have the ceremony at once (*Corr*, II, 299). Despite earlier escapades and unorthodox philosophy,[9] Villiers had again become sometime after 1885 a loyal son of the Church, even expunging from his writings heresies borrowed from Hegelianism, occultism, and illusionism.[10] No wonder he listened to the priest. Yet, even while the necessary documents were being obtained and the letter of the law carried out, Villiers had at least one moment of hesitation. It was only on 14 August 1889 at four o'clock in the afternoon that the wedding was actually performed. From all these proceedings two people were curiously absent. In all likelihood, Jean Marras, who ranked with Mallarmé as Villiers' best friend, stayed away from Paris because he wanted nothing to do with the marriage *in extremis*.[11] On the other hand, it seems that Léon Bloy was excluded by Villiers, who remained on cold terms with him after the Belgian tour, or by Huysmans, who knew Bloy to be opposed to the marriage.

For four days more, Villiers lay dying. No longer did his hand throw back the lock of hair that was constantly falling over his broad forehead; no longer did he tug and twist at his pointed beard.[12] Scarcely capable of movement, but lucid until the end, he worried about Totor, left along with Albert in Nogent; he thought with horror about dying in a hospital. Perhaps he also thought of contemplated yet unfinished works (*Le Vieux de la montagne*, to mention but one), of a literary mission he had only partially fulfilled, or maybe of the play *Axël*, which he was still revising. Did he take solace in the fact that his death would assure Marie and Totor's survival? Or was he simply thinking of eternity? Who can say? In any event, at eleven o'clock on the evening of 18 August 1889, death came peacefully: Villiers asked Marie to hold him and he yielded up his spirit. Three days later, on 21 August, under a torrential rain, a small cortege made its way to Batignolles cemetery, where the body of Villiers de l'Isle-Adam was laid to rest.

II   Contes cruels

Villiers' tales had been appearing piecemeal since 1867, but it was only in 1883 that they were published collectively as *Contes cruels*. Of the twenty-eight tales in the volume, nineteen had been published between 1867 and 1879 (see above, pp. 55–62, 82–98). Most of these had gone through several publications and revisions, and Villiers again submitted them to correction before including them in the volume. If the changes in many only affected details, those in "L'Intersigne," "L'Annonciateur" ("Azraël"), and "Le Secret de l'ancienne musique" ("Le Chapeau chinois") were more substantial.[13] The remaining nine stories were conceived after 1880, and three in fact had no publication prior to the appearance of the collection.

Of the works written after 1880, three satirize the bourgeoisie and the materialism of the age. "Deux Augures," for instance, is a conversation between a supposed aspiring journalist and a newspaper director. The latter rejects the young man's article as too good in the democratic era when "Above all, [have] no genius!" (*CC*, 34) and "Be mediocre" (45) are the rules of the game. While based on reality—the journalist embodying characteristics of Villiers, the director those of publishing magnate Emile de Girardin—the story assumes the proportions of caricature, and the director becomes a symbol of the "lucrative cynicism of the powerful press."[14] In "Fleurs de ténèbres" (1880), Villiers satirizes the practicality and emotional insensitivity of his contemporaries, who even resell flowers used at funerals, so they do not "wither *uselessly* on the fresh tombs" (*CC*, 179). The satire of "Les Brigands" (1882) is particularly truculent. The landowners of Nayrac join forces to go collect their rents, although they know the rumors of highway robbers are false. On their way home, they meet landlords of neighboring Pibrac, who have also banded together. Imagining the tenants' stories to be true, each group mistakes the other for bandits. A battle to save "their lives and their money" (*CC*, 194) results in a general massacre. The tale ends with "the real brigands (that is, the half-dozen poor devils guilty, at most, of having taken a few crusts . . .)" collecting the money from the dead bodies and fleeing across the border (195). In ridiculing the bourgeoisie's fear of the popular classes and its desire to defend its possessions at any cost, Villiers uses three interesting satiric devices. First, the characters are drawn in caricatural terms. Then, he describes the landlords' departure in language that parodies chivalric epics. "Our heroes" (193), he writes, were singing a "heroic song" (192), while "the ladies," their wives, "were looking in admiration at these modern paladins and stuffing their pockets with cough drops" (191). Finally, it is with sheer irony that the landowners, knowing the falsity of the rumors, fall victim to the tenants' stories and mistake their counterparts for robbers.

"Duke of Portland" is a tale of mystery and suspense, partially based on the historic William Bentinck, fifth duke of Portland (1800–1879).[15] After returning to England from the East, Lord Richard abruptly retires to a solitary existence in the family manor. Queen Victoria, who has sent inquiries to the recluse, shudders when she reads a letter from him, while Héléna, the queen's reader, who is betrothed to Portland, falls into a faint. A year later, while the elite of English aristocracy gather at Portland for one of the seasonal balls given but not attended by the duke, this mysterious character, masked, wrapped in a cloak, and preceded by a page ringing a bell, makes his way to the beach. There, he meets Héléna, bids her farewell until next they meet, and dies. Three days later, true to his memory and hopeful of reunion in eternity, Héléna takes the veil. Only at the end, as the narrative returns to the moment of the tale's beginning, does Villiers clarify the mystery. In the East, the noble Richard contracted leprosy by charitably visiting one of its victims and shaking his hand.

"Vox populi" (1880, 1881) is a poetic tale consisting of three

scenes and a conclusion. In the first scene (*CC*, 28–30), set in 1868
during the Second Empire, the people have gathered to see the
"grand review on the Champs-Elysées that day" of Napoleon's anniversary (28). Amid the cheers is heard the melodic plea of a beggar: "Have pity on a poor blind man, if you please!" (30). The second
scene (30–31), set in 1870 during the Third Republic, also depicts a
"grand review on the Champs-Elysées that day" (30), the crowd's
applause, and the beggar's prayer (31). Another "grand review on
the Champs-Elysées that day" (31) is presented in scene three
(31–32), set in 1871 during and after the Commune. The same action
occurs. The masses cheer a leader; the beggar, eyes raised toward
heaven, whimpers: "Have pity on a poor blind man, if you please!"
(32). The repetition of the same action at different historical periods,
the use of identical words to open and close the three scenes, and
the tale's conclusion (32–33) underline the repetitive nature of history and its immutable truths. The people, eager to give their allegiance, are forever intellectually blind. By contrast, the seer,
symbolized by a blind beggar who, like Claire Lenoir, is privy to
eternal truths, understands their real desires. Unfortunately, advice
given by the "Speaker of the people's secret thoughts" (31) constantly goes unheeded. The story's title, referring to the Latin slo-
gan "Vox populi, vox Dei" ("The voice of the people is the voice of
God"), is meant ironically.

The three remaining works, less easily classified, present pictures
of cruel individuals. "Le Désir d'être un homme" (1882), for instance, is a bizarre psychological study of an aging actor, Esprit
Chaudval, who, after impersonating other people for so long, desires to experience an emotion of his own and "be a man" (*CC*, 172).
In hopes of feeling remorse, he sets a fire that claims nearly a
hundred victims. But he is disappointed, for, a victim of his acting
profession, he can feel no emotion of his own, "no menacing phantom" (177). "La Reine Ysabeau" (1880), a pseudohistorical narrative
set in the early fifteenth century, draws a portrait of the wife of
France's King Charles VI (1368–1422). Having learned that her
favorite, Vidame de Maulle, has wagered that he can seduce
Bérénice Escabala, Queen Ysabeau cunningly has him accused of
arson and condemned to death. On the eve of the execution,
Maulle's heroic lawyer changes places with the condemned man,
who escapes in the former's dress. The exchange makes no difference to Ysabeau. To erase Maulle's name "from the list of the living,

she order[s] the sentence to be carried out *anyway*" (*CC* 205).
"Maryelle," a tale within a tale, satirically depicts a courtesan who
sees no contradiction between her need to accept gentlemen's
favors and her fidelity, "in thought as in sensations" (*CC*, 261), to
her young lover Raoul.

We can now make several concluding remarks about this collection. The tales as a whole bear the heavy imprint of the author. The
noble Portland and the young writer of "Deux Augures" are projec-
tions of himself; Maryelle is surely based on one of the society
women he had met. "Vox populi" contains memories of parades on
the Champs-Elysées. Yet these experiences are transformed,
through symbols and poetic imagination, to another level of meaning. Behind almost all the stories is the idea of the nobility of
idealism ("Véra," "Duke of Portland," "L'Intersigne"), the inhu-
manity of positivism and bourgeois values ("Les Demoiselles de
Bienfilâtre," "Deux Augures," "L'Affichage céleste," "Les Brigands"), or the unceasing conflict between the two ("Vox populi,"
"Virginie et Paul," "Sentimentalisme"). The choice of the collection's title is a happy one, for cruelty, either in the situation described or in the mordant satiric style employed, is a feature common to virtually all the stories.[16] Now some tales, like "L'Appareil
pour l'analyse chimique du dernier soupir" or "La Machine à
gloire," may disappoint us because they lack subtlety; others, like
"Fleurs de ténèbres," because they are undeveloped. And the
inclusion of seven poems from his earlier works seems an outright
mistake: Although arranged to present a series of emotions and
collectively called "Conte d'amour" (1880), the poems hardly constitute a tale. Nevertheless, one still has to agree with Mallarmé that
the collection contains "a sum of extraordinary Beauty" (*Corr*, II,
41). No wonder the *Contes cruels* established Villiers as a leader of
the literary avant-garde in the eyes of the younger generation. No
wonder, too, that the volume still haunts us today.

III   L'Eve future

This novel, in six books, takes place at the laboratory of the
American inventor Thomas Edison in Menlo Park, New Jersey,
twenty-five leagues from New York. Edison's lament that his
"phonograph and [he] arrive[d] too late" (*OC*, I, 29) to record the
significant events of history is interrupted by a dispatch, transmitted
from New York: Lord Ewald, who once saved the inventor's life,

will be arriving unexpectedly that night. A similar lament about photography is interrupted by the arrival of the young Englishman, who has come to shake Edison's hand before ending his unhappy existence. Incapable of breaking with a beautiful actress, Alicia Clary, he is likewise incapable of loving the "bourgeois Goddess" (73), whose celestial form is in complete disaccord with her soulless, witless being. Book One ends as Edison promises to save Lord Ewald's life as he once saved his.

In his "magical realm" (104), the "Wizard of Menlo Park" (5, 322) has created a wondrous robot that gives every illusion of human life. By reincarnating Alicia's exterior qualities in Hadaly, Edison will create for Ewald the ideal woman (hence the robot's name, which in Persian signifies ideal), whose form will perfectly mirror her inner being. Ewald has only to lend credence to her existance (136). After some hesitation, the Englishman consents to the experiment, and in Book Three the two descend to an "underground Eden" (179), Hadaly's abode. There Edison reveals that the suicide of his friend Anderson over the "dull chimera" (241) Evelyn Habel (whose name suggests vanity) and a desire to save other men from a similar fate motivated him to create the android. He further reveals that he has been waiting for someone desperate enough to undergo the first experiment (Book Four). Then Edison explains the mechanics of Hadaly—her four surfaces, her wires, her lungs consisting of two phonographs of gold, a cylinder on which are recorded her gestures, her systems of locomotion and balance—and the manner in which Alicia's exterior will be reproduced in her (Book Five).

In the final book, Alicia arrives from New York. At the end of three weeks, Edison, assisted by Mistress Any Sowana, has so perfectly copied the actress's features that Lord Ewald mistakes Hadaly for her. At first angered at being duped (373), he rejects the robot (388–89); then, he realizes it is not Hadaly, but "the living [Alicia] that is the phantom" (394). He will take the former with him to England aboard *The Wonderful*. Having placed Hadaly in the coffin wherein she will be transported, Edison reveals to Ewald one further secret: Sowana is in fact a spirit liberated through hypnotism from the body of Anderson's cataleptic widow and is now inhabiting Hadaly. After Ewald's departure, Edison discovers that Mistress Anderson, deprived of her soul, has "left the world of humans" (422). The novel ends with news of a fire on board *The Wonderful* and a telegram from Ewald confirming the loss of Hadaly.

The origin of this long and complex novel has been much debated. Some critics claim that the novel was inspired by Poe,[17] others, by Goethe or Eliphas Lévi.[18] Some critics, following Pontavice's lead, claim that a certain Englishman and a conversation one night in a restaurant gave birth to the story.[19] Still others maintain that it resulted from Villiers' passion in 1874 for the shallow and unworthy Anna Eyre;[20] this theory is all the more plausible, they contend, if one remembers that Villiers began the novel in 1877 (or 1878) and published an incomplete version in 1880–1881, even though the definitive text dates from 1885–1886.[21]

Whatever the origin of the idea, Villiers has transformed it into a novel as ambiguous, as rich and varied in significance, as the robot itself.[22] On its most basic level, *L'Eve future* can be looked at as a social satire.[23] Through the mouth of the sceptical but nostalgic Edison, Villiers satirizes a humanity that has foresaken "all the beliefs that so many thousand heroes, thinkers, and martyrs had bequeathed [to it]" for an unshakable faith in progress, for, as he says, "the smoke that comes from a boiler" (320). He also has Edison ridicule human pretense (258–59), the emptiness of human conversations where "every word is and can only be an unnecessary repetition" (265), and the vacuity of certain feminine types (220–26, 235–40). Moreover, the author incorporates in the person of Alicia all the characteristics of the bourgeoisie he so abhorred—the cult of common sense (81), insensitivity to art (84, 92, 334), stupidity (85, 339), practicality (86), obsession with money (337)—and demonstrates that one can reasonably prefer a robot to her.

On another level, the novel can be read as a symbolic illustration of Villiers' illusionistic theories. To convince Lord Ewald of the possibility of curing his painful love, Edison demonstrates that nothing is knowable except one's thoughts—all else is illusion. What Ewald really loves is an Alicia created by his own imagination: "The being that you love in the living, and which, for you *alone* is REAL, is not at all the one that *appears* in this human passer-by, but the one of your Desire" (135). In a sense, Ewald has replaced Alicia's mediocre soul with an ideal truth. Consequently, what Edison will do, in response to Ewald's desperate plea (89), is to separate Alicia's body from her soul by reincarnating the exterior, without the mediocre soul, in the robot (126). Ewald will then fill the empty form with his ideal, and the robot will "vivify" the ideal he loves (135).[24] This "joint presence" (136) will be "no less real for him than a flesh-and-blood woman," or for that matter, any other element of the material world.[25] Hadaly's existence, like everything else's, depends entirely on Ewald's believing in her: "Illusion for illusion, the Being . . . called Hadaly depends on the free volition of one who WILL DARE to conceive it . . ." (136).[26] Knowing Hadaly is Ewald's salvation, the scientist enjoins Ewald to believe in her as he does in other illusions around him: "Affirm [her being], with a little of your strong faith, as you affirm the being . . . of all the illusions that surround you" (136).

As in "Véra," where the apparition resulting exclusively from D'Athol's will at the same time has an objective reality, in this novel, too, Villiers mixes illusionistic theory with notions of the occult and the supernatural.[27] Hadaly's soul is the product of Ewald's imagination, and her existence for him does depend on his belief in her. Yet it is no less true that Sowana, the spirit liberated from Mistress Anderson's body, exists objectively and animates the robot. The spirits from the beyond whose calls and responses Sowana interprets (375–87, 390–92) likewise have a reality independent of Ewald's mind.

On another level, then, L'Eve future can be read as a profession of faith in the supernatural and an attempt to convince others of its existence, purportedly by scientific means. As in "Claire Lenoir," Villiers turns against the positivists the weapons they themselves used to cast doubt and aspersions on a supernatural beyond.[28] Through the science of hypnotism—it is known Villiers frequented a Dr. Latino's "soirées of hypnotism and spiritualism" around 1880 (Corr, II, 8–9)—Edison liberates a mysterious being from a cataleptic body, and the robot he builds, employing the latest scientific technology, becomes the point of contact between man and spirits from the beyond. Science is not necessarily antithetical to the mysterious, as the positivists (like Bonhomet) would have it. In the hands of the enlightened Edison, "artist translated into . . . scientist" (OC, I, 12), it is shown to confirm the supernatural and actually becomes the "auxiliary of dream."[29]

Finally, the novel can be read on a metaphysical level. The world, as Edison points out, is totally discontinuous. There is disjuncture between matter and sense, no correspondence between reality and man's conception of it, and in Alicia, the woman created by God, complete antithesis between body and soul. The situation is intolerable to man and causes him incalcuable suffering. Lord Ewald is

even driven to suicide. What Edison proposes is to create a new
continuity by taking the old discontinuity to its logical conclusion.
Disjuncture already exists between body and soul. Why not then
complete the rupture by separating definitively the two elements,
by removing Alicia's mediocre soul from her celestial body?[30] Why
not create through science a new Eve to replace the imperfect one
God made? In an effort to aid mankind, Edison attempts no less
than to rival God in his creation and reverse the order established
by him. Ewald understands fully the nature of Edison's revolt for he
says: "To undertake the creation of such a being . . . would be to
tempt . . . *God"* (130).

To underline the element of revolt in Edison's act, Villiers alludes
to two myths in the course of the novel. The first is that of Prome-
theus (135, 252). Like this god, who defied Zeus by stealing fire to
benefit mankind, Edison challenges God by designing a woman
more beneficial to man than the one he created. The second myth
Villiers invokes is that of Faust. Not only does he mention Goethe's
Faust in the preface (6) and take two epigraphs from the work (181,
319), he also refers to Berlioz's *Faust* (194) and the opera by Charles
Gounod of the same name (202). Moreover, the title of the second
book, "The Pact," is clearly an allusion to this legend. Like Mephistopheles of the myth, Edison offers help to Ewald, who like Faust is
on the point of suicide. Like Faust and Mephistopheles, Ewald and
Edison conclude a pact. It is true that, unlike Faust, Ewald is not
obliged to sell his soul, but he does promise Edison to live an
additional twenty-one days. The parallels are not strict, but one
thing is clear: Edison and Ewald's attempt to create scientifically a
new Eve is as much a revolt against the divine order as the alliance
of Faust and Mephistopheles.[31]

This revolt against God by Edison does not succeed. In the last
chapter, as the epigraph "Poenituit autem Deus . . ." implies (423),
God intervenes and punishes those who have defied his laws by
destroying the robot. Edison is left shuddering, in Raitt's words,
from "fear and horror in the face of an implacable deity that permits
no alleviation of the sufferings it inflicts on humanity."[32] What
significance can we attribute to this ending, especially in view of the
earlier parts of the novel? One recalls that Villiers completed most
of *L'Eve future* between 1879 and 1880, a period of great frustration
and unhappiness for him. No doubt he shared Ewald's sense of
despair. No doubt, too, he would have liked to topple the world

order and set it aright as Edison attempts to do.[33] Despite the subsequent revisions to attenuate its impact,[34] the early part of the novel still reflects the frustration, anger, and defiance Villiers felt toward the end of the 1870s. On the other hand, the last chapter, about God's intervention, was probably written about 1885, when Villiers was beset by religious scruples. Its composition was doubtlessly motivated by a desire to bring the novel into closer line with his refound orthodoxy and no doubt encouraged by his friend Léon Bloy, somewhat of a religious hard-liner.

From the novel's multiplicity of meaning, we turn to two esthetic problems in the work. The first is the use of scientific description. To make the novel plausible and to have the reader accept the extraordinary as possible, Villiers sets out to blur the neat distinction between possible-impossible and reality-dream existing in the reader's mind. For instance, the creation of an ideal woman is fantastic, but Villiers anchors the novel in reality by specifying places, dates, times, and distances. The fantasy introduced into the realistic framework takes on a borrowed believability. His choice of Thomas Edison as protagonist is another attempt to confuse the reader. Edison was of course a historical person (1847–1931), still living and working at the time of the novel's publication. Thus, despite Villiers' avowal that his character is "at least passably distinct from reality" (6), one may well confuse him with the person and take as true the most extraordinary actions of the character. Scientific descriptions play an analogous function in the novel. The robot, Sowana's liberation from Mistress Anderson, the reproduction of Alicia's features in Hadaly, and the realm beyond are described with the same technical precision and detail as the telephone. We forget the boundaries of science-imagination and come close to accepting the robot, Edison's experiments, and the beyond as scientific phenomena on a par with the phone.

Although the scientific description has a distinct purpose, use of it is not very adroit. Substantially less description would have sufficed to confuse the lines of science-imagination in the reader's mind. Villiers loses all sense of measure and unnecessarily overloads the novel. The excess has dilatorious consequences. Details become wearisome, the work grows heavy, and Book Five, one long explanation of Hadaly's internal parts, has as much force as a dead weight. Worst of all, the philosophical and metaphysical interest of the novel frequently gets lost in the barrage of pseudoscientific facts.

The second problem concerns Edison's philosophical meditations at the beginning of the novel (16–20, 25–29, 38–48). There is no doubt that these passages fulfill an important function in the work. Like Chapter Four, where Sowana's disincarnated voice is heard, and Chapter Eight, where attention is drawn to Hadaly's detached arm, the meditations, emphasizing as they do a separation of sound from object or meaning from sound, are designed to introduce the theme of discontinuity and Edison's attempt to rectify the discordant universe.[35] But here, as with Villiers scientific descriptions, the question of proportion must be raised. Were twenty pages of reflection really necessary to foreshadow a theme, especially since Chapters Four and Eight effectively do the same thing? As it is, these pages retard the novel's beginning and weigh it down with cumbersome baggage. Less philosophy would have added more to the work.

In a letter to Jean Marras, Villiers once marveled about the "perseverance in the analyses . . . [and] the astounding strokes of imagination" found in *L'Eve future* (*Corr*, I, 262). While I agree that the novel displays endless imagination and originality, I also think Villiers has persevered to a fault in some of his analyses. If there is anything that prevents the work from becoming "immortal" (*Corr*, I, 262), it is the lengthy scientific and philosophical discussions, which paralyze the novel and exhaust the reader.

IV   Akëdysséril

The long prose poem *Akëdysséril* (1886) can be divided into three parts. The first part (*OC*, V, 229–40) sets the stage for the appearance of the Hindu monarch Akëdysséril. A panorama of the holy city Benares, anxiously awaiting her victorious return from battle, is followed by a retrospective view of her rise to power. Born the daughter of a shepherd, she became queen of Benares, thanks to love. After her husband's death, to ensure power for herself, she imprisoned Prince Sedjnour, next in line to the throne, and his fiancée Yelka in two palaces separated by the Ganges River. This part ends with final preparations in the city and the arrival of the advance guard. A description of the sacred, avoided avenue leading to the temple of Shiva foreshadows events about to take place there. Part Two (240–50) paints Akëdysséril's long-awaited arrival, preceded by her entourage, and her abrupt departure from the city's central plaza. Having glanced at the temple and consulted her in-

formers, the monarch races her chariot, to the crowd's consterna-
tion, down the sacred avenue. Part Three (250–83) takes place in the
temple of Shiva. Once inside, the monarch sees the colossus of the
god, the immolation stone, and Shiva's high pontiff, a seer whose
ascetic discipline has resulted in superhuman power and an understanding of the universe's secrets. She asks the pontiff why in her
absence he has betrayed her. To prevent further civil war and re-
bellion, the monarch consented to Sedjnour and Yelka's death, provided the seer could bring about death by an augmentation of their
love, by "a joy so intense, so penetrating, still so unfelt, that this
death would seem to them more desirable than life" (261). Relying
on her informers' testimony, she suspects that the seer has coaxed
them to death by arousing jealousy, feelings of abandonment, and
sadness. The pontiff shows her the bodies. The "imprint of ideal joy"
on the lovers' faces convinces her that "a supernatural felicity . . .
had to deliver them from life" (278–79). The ecstasy of the union the
seer withheld and then granted carried them away. A bit envious of
their love, the monarch sheds two tears. Then she announces the
death to officers standing in the temple's entrance and asks that
prayers be said for the royal couple.

Despite Hindu trappings and the Oriental setting, the principal
themes of the tale are familiar to Villiers' readers. The theme of the
seer whose extraordinary knowledge and power derive from ab-
stention from worldly pleasures has already been seen in *Isis* and
"L'Annonciateur." Love here, as in *L'Eve future*, is depicted as an
illusion, a mental state created by the mind, that is always susceptible to the destructive force of reality. While Sedjnour and Yelka
live, their love endures because they live separated from the world
and from each other. In contrast, while her husband lived, Akëdysséril's love for him, as the seer says, was threatened by earthly
ambition: "Already favored with a scepter, your mind troubled by
ambitious dreams, your soul scattered by a thousand future cares, it
was no longer in your power to give yourself completely" (274–75).
Sedjnour and Yelka die from fulfillment of their desires, an unexpected union. But the cruel fact is that once they have been brought
together, death is really, as in *Le Prétendant*, the only way to preserve that love. Had they lived, the real Sedjnour would pale before
the image Yelka fashioned of him, as Yelka would pale before the
image Sedjnour made of her. Perfect love would wither before a
painful disappointment. In Villiers' own words, "the torture would

have been, for them, to survive this unequaled moment" of en-counter (280).

If one can take his words literally, Edouard Dujardin, director of the *Revue wagnerienne*, was so impressed with this work that he completely forgot his editorial duties and instead reread the "wonder *Akëdysséril*" (*Corr*, II, 131). There is much here that is impressive. The local color, perhaps borrowed from Matthew Atmore Sherring's *The Sacred City of the Hindus* (1868), is frequently dazzling.[36] The language, with its onomatopoetic evocations— "Soudain, l'on entendit les sourds bruissements des tymbrils mêlés à des cliquetis d'armes et de chaînes—et, brisées par les chocs sonores des cymbales" (*OC*, V, 237), to cite but one example[37]—is at times powerful. Furthermore, the beginning of Part Two, reminiscent of "L'Annonciateur," is skillfully organized to suggest the progressive approach of the main character. The avant-garde first arrives (237), then the royal entourage (240–42). In the distance is seen a black elephant on which the monarch's form soon becomes visible (242). Finally, Akëdysséril's sublime face is recognized by all (244). To create symmetry and counterbalance the beginning, the end of Part Two is arranged to suggest Akëdysséril's fading into the distance. The people "soon see her fade away" (249). Then they "indistinctly see her" stop her horses and climb the dreaded stairs (249). Finally, she disappears into the temple (250).

Despite these obvious merits, I cannot completely share Dujardin's enthusiasm. One problem with the work is that the descriptions are at times trite, as calling the sun the "world's phoenix" (229), or even nonsensical, as describing the East as "occidental" (229).[38] Another, perhaps graver, problem is the quantity of description. The plot of the tale is simple. Yet the work runs over fifty pages. It takes ten pages to describe the expectant city, another fifteen to introduce Akëdysséril, while her complaint to the high priest alone takes seventeen pages. Regretfully, a sense of balance between story and description that Villiers struck in the shorter "Impatience de la foule" and "L'Annonciateur" is here lost. The unfortunate result is that description overwhelms the narrative and, rather than delighting, tires and bores the reader.

V Tribulat Bonhomet

Tribulat Bonhomet first appeared in the early "Claire Lenoir" (1867). Although Villiers never ceased thinking about his character, it was only later, probably prompted by publicity from *A Rebours* (1884), that he wrote additional stories about him. A collection of tales entitled *Tribulat Bonhomet* was published in 1887. This includes a slightly modified "Claire Lenoir"—because of religious scruples, Villiers now makes Hegelian Césaire less sympathetic and his heroine, formerly a theistic Hegelian, a Christian[39]—preceded by three shorter works and followed by an epilogue.

The first tale, "Le Tueur de cygnes," describes in the third person how Bonhomet, "that modern valiant knight" (*OC*, III, 20), sometimes rises at midnight, dons his gauntlets "from some medieval armor" (17), and makes his way to a swan sanctuary. After lying in wait, he achieves the goal of the trip. He traps the "artists," the "bird-poets" (19, 20, 21), strangles them, and delights in their euphonious death song, this being the only sound that helps him endure "the deceptions of life" (15).

The tale is obviously making a statement about the diabolical cruelty of Bonhomet and the bourgeoisie he represents. But to understand the full implications of Bonhomet's activity, the tale must be read symbolically. The description of the swans as "bird-poets" and "artists" indeed suggests such an interpretation. Because of their mellifluous voices, their white bodies, and their seclusion, the swans are apt symbols for artists who, living apart from the world, unsullied by its materialism, devote their life to the creation of beauty. Without really understanding art—Bonhomet "musically esteemed only the peculiar sweetness *of the tone* of these symbolic voices" (20)—the bourgeois invade this sacred domain. Not unlike the sailors in Baudelaire's "L'Albatros" (1859), they subject artists to any humiliation or cruelty to satisfy their own selfish ends. At the hands of society, artists suffer a real martyrdom. The story's bleakness is only tempered by the description of Bonhomet. Picturing him as a knight who goes forth in warrior's garb to defend noble principles, Villiers makes us laugh by the heroic terms he uses, applicable to the medieval knight but totally inappropriate to an insensitive, satanic man.

In "La Motion du Dr Tribulat Bonhomet," Villiers records the proposal supposedly made to the French legislature by the bourgeois doctor after news of horrible earthquakes in the south. To submit "these jolts to the brakes of a sound control" (*OC*, III, 27), Bonhomet suggests that buildings be put on the spot most in danger and that artists be invited to live in them. When the tremor occurs, these believers in the mysterious, dangerous to society, will be destroyed, rather than honorable burghers. Suspicious of artists and fearful of the irrational, Bonhomet is as concerned with giving meaning to the "interventions of the Absurd" (31) as with ridding the world of artists. No wonder he delights in his proposal. The earthquakes will be given meaning and purpose at the same time as his enemies are eliminated legally.

"Le Banquet des Eventualistes" returns to a theme we have already seen in "Les Brigands": the bourgeoisie's fear of the proletariat. Here, however, the theme is treated more comically. To allay fears of popular insurrection, shared by his fellow "Eventualists" (a name coined to designate those with "possible certitudes" [*OC*, III, 41]), Bonhomet recalls with relish a measure the government has supposedly adopted to prevent trouble among the impoverished masses. A decree permits the cabarets, cafés, and taverns of the capital to remain open until two o'clock in the morning (38). As a result, the populace, which expends all its energy in late night partying, is only too glad to postpone its uprising. In fifteen years, "one thus obtains an exemplary population of visionaries, whose physical and moral strength becomes diluted" (39). The measure is ingenious: "It paralyzes in *advance*, without bloodshed and in a bourgeois way, all sedition" (40).

Following "Claire Lenoir," the collection ends with an epilogue entitled "Les Visions merveilleuses du Dr Tribulat Bonhomet." The scare Bonhomet experienced twenty years earlier, recounted in "Claire Lenoir," has heightened his nervous condition. He engages Fructuence as a wet-nurse, and when her milk does not produce the promised cure, he keeps her on as a housekeeper. Together, they leave Paris for Bonhomet's country house in Digne. The earthquakes and cyclones in the vicinity, however, aggravate the doctor's condition and he takes to bed. Impudently pardoning God for faults done him, he falls into a faint that makes some reporters think he is dead. But he soon awakens, alarmed by the strange visions he has had. In the visions, abounding in bad puns, an angry God chastises Bonhomet's doubt, stinginess, and immorality and then, exasperated with his flippancy, sends him back "among the jokers" (*OC*, III, 218).

In judging the collection as a whole, it is apparent that the tales are not of consistent quality. By its insights, intrigue, and development, "Claire Lenoir" is vastly superior to the other tales. Only "Le

Tueur de cygnes" comes close to equaling its impact. "La Motion"
and "Le Banquet" are really not stories at all but satiric essays, and
"Les Visions merveilleuses" is seriously flawed by its banal play on
words. Furthermore, one reasonably expects the central character
of a collection of tales to be consistent and to impart a certain unity
to the work. But that, unfortunately, is not the case here. The
Tribulat of "Claire Lenoir" is skeptical, bigoted, and comical; there
is little humorous about him in the tales composed later. He destroys swans, he proposes to exterminate artists, he gloats that the
proletariat will drink itself into dullness, and he attacks poor Fructuence. He is actively satanic. This development of character may
be interesting, but it destroys the unity of the collection, especially
since Bonhomet is less developed in "Claire Lenoir" than in the
three tales that are placed before it. Rather than displaying an expected progression, *Tribulat Bonhomet* is marked by a veritable
regression.[40]

VI *Other Tales*

After the brilliance of the *Contes cruels*, Villiers' later collections—*L'Amour   suprême*   (1886),   *Histoires   insolites*   (1888),
Nouveaux Contes cruels (1888)—are somewhat disappointing. Many
works in the first two volumes, like "Les Expériences du D^r
Crookes," about supposed scientific experiments confirming the occult, are long and rambling. Others suffer from lack of action; "La
Maison du bonheur" is really a description of two elect souls who
flee a vulgar world. Narratives like "Le Droit du passé," "Le Tzar et
les grands-ducs," and "Une Entrevue à Solesmes" are personal and
historical anecdotes rather than imagined tales. Furthermore, of the
eight *Nouveaux Contes cruels*, most are derivative. Four are based on
borrowed material,[41] while three repeat, with little variation,
themes and techniques of earlier tales. "Les Amies de pension," for
instance, recalls "Les Demoiselles de Bienfilâtre," as "Le Chant du
coq" recalls "L'Annonciateur." And if "L'Amour du naturel" is about
the effects of materialism on life, not just love, it calls to mind the
earlier "Virginie et Paul" by its idyllic setting, dialogue, and characters whose names are borrowed from other literary works.

Nevertheless, the three collections contain some notable excep-
tions, and in these Villiers attains the high artistic level of the
Contes cruels. "L'Amour suprême," after which the collection of
1886 is named, is a story of supreme love fulfilled in death. After

claiming that people have been willing to "sacrifice kisses [and] forego embraces" to avoid "the unfulfilled hopes" and "illusions of worldly love" (*OC*, V, 9), the narrator illustrates the idea with his own experience. During a ball at the Ministry of Foreign Affairs, he unexpectedly met Lysiane d'Aubelleyne, whom he had known and loved years ago in Brittany. About to flee the "tangible world where we ourselves are only appearances" (20), she came that night only to affront, according to Carmelite custom, "the world's temptations before professing her vows" (22). She consented to see the narrator once again the following morning in the chapel of Notre-Dame-des-Champs. When he arrived, a priest was reciting the mass of the dead. The white-draped bier, candles, and nuns indicated that an induction ceremony was to take place. He now realized Mlle d'Aubelleyne had invited him to witness the profession of her vows, her dying to the world. Toward the ceremony's end, her eyes met his. Their love, like that of Portland and Héléna, will be fulfilled in death, for in her eyes he read the promise of an "eternal rendez-vous" (30).

Although the narrator is surprised by this outcome, Villiers' imagery has in fact prepared the reader. Mlle d'Aubelleyne's purity and death to the world is reflected the moment we see her in her pale complexion, her eyes "of white lilies," and the black dress decorated with lilies (16–17). Her comparison to Beatrice (14), whose love from afar raised Dante's own to a spiritual dimension, suggests the role she will play at the end, where, incidentally, the image is repeated and developed (30). The tolling of midnight, foreshadowing the death bell of the religious ceremony (28), suggests a future death as Villiers compares it to a "formless bird of wind, sonorous echoes and darkness" (19). Finally, the meeting of Mlle d'Aubelleyne and the narrator on a balcony, detached from the clamor of the worldly gathering, facing the eternal stars, foreshadows their eventual meeting beyond the sense world, in eternity.

True love and its incompatibility with the world are also the theme of "Les Amants de Tolède" *(Histoires insolites)*. To preserve an innocent couple's love from the onslaught of disillusioning reality, Tomas de Torquemada, the grand inquisitor of Spain, submits them to what he calls the "trial by Happiness" (*OC*, VI, 145). Binding them naked, setting them upon the marriage bed, he leaves them alone "to their immense joy" (144). Their purity permits them to experience absolute love. After they are unbound, however, they have no desire to repeat the incident. Henceforth, they live almost separately in their own apartments, dying without posterity, for they realize that they have experienced a sublime and unique moment and that any attempt to relive it can only be a disappointment.

Four satiric tales from the collections are worth noting. The first, "Le Secret de l'échafaud" (*L'Amour suprême*), is based on contemporary executions, experimentation with the dead, and two historical characters, Dr. Edmond-Désiré Couty de La Pommerais and Dr. Armand Velpeau.[42] La Pommerais, who is awaiting execution for murder, receives a visit from Velpeau. After indicating that a much-debated point is whether conscious life persists in the brain after decapitation, the latter proposes to the former an experiment that will resolve the question. After the blade falls, La Pommerais is to wink his right eye three times if he is aware of life. La Pommerais agrees, and moments after the execution, Velpeau anxiously leans over the severed head to observe the results. The right eye, however, winks only once. The inscrutable sign and the inconclusive result of the experiment make the point of the satire clear. Life and death are enigmas. In vain, cruel experimenters like Velpeau poke, prod, and profane the dead; science is incapable of answering the fundamental questions of life.

"L'Héroïsme du docteur Hallidonhill" (*Histoires insolites*) is about a London physician who offhandedly prescribes a dubious cure—a stay in Nice and a diet of watercress—to a skeleton of a patient, for whom he has already given up all hope. When after six months the skeleton returns a giant, Hallidonhill does not hesitate to sacrifice to science the life he has saved. Grabbing a revolver, he shoots the patient in order to examine the body and explain "the arch-miraculous action of watercress" (*OC*, VI, 82). The point of the satire is clear: Modern-day science, treating men like guinea pigs, is indifferent to human values. But, despite the serious topic, the work is never heavy or morose. Through exaggeration and irony (as in the title itself), the satire not only instructs, it also amuses.

"La Légende de l'éléphant blanc" (*L'Amour suprême*) at first strikes one as being nothing more than an amusing narrative. Out of national pride, Lord W*** hires tamers to capture a legendary white elephant from Burma and transport it back to the London Zoo. Having captured the sacred beast, the tamers dye it black to get it out of the country. They are done in by their own ruse. They cannot remove the dye, and Lord W*** is unwilling to pay for a white elephant that is black (*OC*, V, 123). Behind this literal level, however, lies a symbolic meaning. By its rarity, color, and sacredness, the elephant, like the swans in "Le Tueur de cygnes," represents the artist, that rare person who lives apart from the materialistic world and contemplates the divine. Villiers uses the symbol to satirize the unwillingness of practical men (116) to respect that sacredness and society's desire to exploit the artist, even removing from him his very identity.

"Les Plagiaires de la foudre" *(Histoires insolites)*, a kind of fable, also has a satiric intent. On a Pacific island, a breed of parrots imitate the sound of thunder. By their "talent" (*OC*, VI, 13), they scare the other inhabitants away. Their know-how is nevertheless limited. Try as they may, the "feathered sycophants" (14) cannot imitate the cry of the eagle or the roar of the lion. Clearly, Villiers is ridiculing those writers, who gain some success by imitating mediocre talents but who are at a loss when it comes to a true genius.

Another tale involving the guillotine, "Les Phantasmes de M. Redoux" *(Histoires insolites)*, is worth noting especially for the way it combines satire with terror. At first we are amused by the satirical portrait of Antoine Redoux, esteemed citizen of Paris, typical bourgeois, whose controlled existence prevents him from ever realizing his fantasies. When the slightly inebriated protagonist, in London on business, yields to the fantasy of playing King Louis XVI and gets caught under a guillotine late one night in Madame Tussaud's Wax Museum, our feelings begin to change. Momentarily, out of hatred for everything Redoux represents, we rejoice that his head may at any instant fall under the blade from above. Then, as Villiers suggests the captive's horror by describing external manifestations—chattering of teeth, whitening of hair and beard—desire for revenge leaves us. We identify with the terrified human being, and we imagine ourselves under the unstable blade, waiting for the inevitable.

Finally, there are in these collections two tales of suspense and terror that are superb. The first is "Catalina" *(L'Amour suprême)*. To rest his mind from the study of German philosophy, the narrator of the tale journeys to Spain. In Santander, he meets an old friend, Lieutenant Gérard de Villebreuse, who has just arrived from Guiana and is bringing to the Zoological Museum of Madrid a collection of hummingbirds, orchid bulbs, and a treasure. Discussion of the treasure is interrupted by the appearance of Catalina, a "flower girl of the wharf" (*OC*, V, 139). Suddenly, Gérard remembers that it is the anniversary of his mother's death and that he must return to his ship. He invites his friend to spend the night with Catalina in his hotel room. In the middle of the night, the narrator is awakened by "old wood splitting" (144). From a distant church, midnight sounds. The pendulum, however, seems to be in the room, "successively striking now the masonry of the wall, now the partition of a neighboring room" (145). The wind seems to produce a "hissing of damp wood" (146). The narrator hears people fleeing the hotel and notices Catalina, now awake, shivering and unable to speak. To his cries for explanations, the fleeing occupants retort that he is crazy "to sleep with the Devil in the room!" (147). Igniting a rolled-up newspaper, the narrator spies a gigantic python that has loosened itself from its ropes. He now understands: This is Gérard's treasure, its swinging body has produced the sound of the pendulum, and its tongue the hissing sound. Panic-stricken, the narrator grabs Catalina and flees. Taking a steamer, he returns home immediately, happy to leave "the contingencies of the world of phenomena" (152) for the abstract world of philosophy.

What is ingenious in this tale is the build up of suspense and the intensity of terror. When the narrator first awakes in the hotel room, it is unclear whether the splitting, thumping, and hissing sounds are real or the product of imagination. It is possible that the narrator, like so many characters in Poe, is just an excitable, nervous individual. When people start fleeing, the reader realizes that there is something objective to fear. But what? Although Catalina's teeth are chattering, one wonders whether she is the source of danger, perhaps a person carrying a curse. She is from exotic Havana, and the tale is, after all, named for her. Moreover, the people fleeing the hotel decry the narrator's "sleeping with the Devil in the room" (147), and no one else is ostensibly present. Our fear abates slightly when the narrator lights the newspaper and the unknown danger becomes known. But not for long. Villiers' detailed description of the snake's coils, its swaying body inching closer and closer (reminiscent of the pendulum in Poe's immortal tale), and its darting tongue revivify our terror.

The second tale of terror, "La Torture par l'espérance" *(Nouveaux Contes cruels)*, is also marked by echoes of Poe. Villiers himself seems to acknowledge a debt to the American, for the story bears an epigraph—"Oh! for a voice to speak"—taken from "The Pit and the Pendulum." There is, however, a significant difference between the two tales: If much of the terror in Poe's work derives from the description of the pendulum, the slow inexorable approach of a physical danger, here the terror is provoked more subtly through psychological means. A fear of recapture obsesses the protagonist, and the reader shares the agony.

This tale, in truth, is a masterpiece. Not only is it concise, a little over seventeen hundred words, but the plot is of extreme simplicity. In a first part, the Spanish grand inquisitor announces to heretic Rabbi Aser Abarbanel that tomorrow he will submit to an *auto da fé* (*OC*, III, 237–39). Then, finding his cell unlocked, the rabbi makes his way down a deserted corridor toward freedom (240–45). In a third part, met by the inquisitor, he realizes that "all the stages of this fatal evening were only an arranged torture, that of Hope" (245–47). The tale is a masterpiece, lastly and above all, because it sustains a single impression of terror throughout the entire narrative, right from mention of the inquisitor at the beginning to his reappearance at the end.

These nine tales show that Villiers remained as before a vibrant short story writer. If the proportion of masterpieces in these collections was not as great as in *Contes cruels*, circumstances must be blamed. By the 1880s, with new family responsibilities, Villiers was under more financial pressure to publish than when he wrote most of the earlier tales. At this time, too, he was frequently in bad health. On top of this, he was now well enough known to be able to get almost anything he wrote published. As a result, Villiers filled his collections not solely with imaginative tales but with reminiscences, critical articles, derivative works, and even hastily composed stories. *L'Amour suprême, Histoires insolites,* and *Nouveaux Contes cruels* obviously suffer from this financial pressure and rapid assemblage; so will *Chez les passants,* a collection that Villiers was preparing at the time of his death.

CHAPTER 5

Posthumous Life, Posthumous Works

I Death, Eclipse of Fame, Revival (1889–1970)

SHORTLY before he died, Villiers appointed Mallarmé and Huysmans legal executors and entrusted his papers to them. After his death, the two men not only made funeral arrangements, settled Marie's financial accounts, and got the ministry to pay for Victor's education, they also began sorting Villiers' papers and published in 1890 two works included among them. One was *Axël*, which Villiers had been proofing at the time of his death; the other was *Chez les passants*, a collection of short pieces in prose for which the deceased had signed a contract (*Corr*, II, 270–71). Following the publication of these works, the executors lost patience with the torn, disordered, frequently illegible papers and gladly entrusted poet Rodolphe Darzens, Villiers' friend, with the difficult task of putting them in order.[1] It seems that they even arbitrarily distributed some bundles of manuscripts to Villiers' other friends, such as Remy de Gourmont, for it was through this critic's efforts that the tale "Les Filles de Milton" (*L'Echo de Paris*, 17 February 1891), as well as other fragments (*Mercure de France*, 1890–1891), first appeared. A collection of texts was put together by Darzens and published in 1893 as *Propos d'Au-delà*, a title suggesting an intimation of death that Villiers had once considered using for his *Histoires insolites*. The rest of the papers, including letters, fragments, and ideas for future works, however, remained in Darzens' private possession and went unpublished until after his death in 1938.

As a result of the many necrologies that followed Villiers' death, as well as the publication of *Axël*, *Chez les passants*, and *Propos d'Au-delà*, the writer's fame continued to grow in the early 1890s. This fame was further advanced by a series of lectures that Mallarmé devoted to him in February 1890, biographical articles that Robert du Pontavice collected into a volume (1893), and the republication of several works long out of print. *L'Eve future*, for example, was reprinted in 1890 and was soon followed by *Premières Poésies* (1893), *Morgane* (1894), *Elën* (1896), *La Révolte* (1897), selected tales under the title *Histoires souveraines* (1899), and the early unfinished novel *Isis* (1900).[2] Furthermore, the staging of *Axël* in 1894 and its two successful performances before enthusiastic audiences greatly enhanced Villiers' reputation. In 1895, therefore, when Villiers' remains were transferred from Batignolles, where the plot had only been temporarily consigned, to Père Lachaise Cemetery, friends and admirers could well be pleased. Not only had a final resting place been donated by the city of Paris, but there was good reason to believe that Villiers would be remembered as an important writer of his time.

But this belief was to be disappointed. Already in 1895 there was a subtle hint that Villiers' celebrity was waning. On 14 February, the premiere performance of *Elën* received a cool reception before the audience of the Free Theater. A second ominous sign occurred a year later when a performance of *La Révolte* at the Odéon generated little more enthusiasm. The sudden reversal of opinion that Villiers' reputation underwent sometime after 1895 can only be explained in light of contemporary events. The fact was that the Symbolist movement was disintegrating. Older members of the movement like Mallarmé, Verlaine, and Rodenbach were dying. The younger ones like Remy de Gourmont were turning to new ideas and new modes of expression, and as they renounced the Symbolist esthetic, they began to censure the works they had once revered as prophetic. They singled out for special criticism Villiers' style and his excessive disdain for life. The public went along with these judgments, and by 1900, the reaction against idealist literature and Villiers' work in particular was so widespread that the author was hardly ever mentioned any more in literary circles.[3]

Villiers was not to be forgotten, however, and interest in his work would stage a revival. Studies devoted to him by Alexis von Kraemer (1900), H. Chapoutot (1908), E. de Rougemont (1910), and Fernand Clerget (1913) were published early in the twentieth century. Unfortunately, von Kraemer's thesis in Swedish was not accessible to many, and none of the studies dealt at length with Villiers' works or the influence he exerted on other writers. In the 1930s, Villiers gained new attention from Surrealists as well as from critics interested in Symbolism as a historical movement. The publication of his works in eleven volumes was completed by Mercure de France (1931), and major studies by E. Drougard (1931, 1935, 1936) and Max Daireaux (1936), stressing Villiers' writings, appeared. But, while noting in an article commemorating the centennial of Villiers' birth (1938) that "his name often comes up in books and articles . . . attached [as he is] to the history of Symbolism," one critic still wondered whether people really read Villiers' books.[4] In less than twenty years this situation was to change, for by 1956 another critic noted that "one could well speak of a revival, not only of Villiers studies, but of general interest in his work."[5] In the last fifteen years interest in the French-speaking world has continued to grow. Not only has Raitt's landmark book on Villiers been published (1965), much attention has also been paid to Villiers' neglected works. Thanks to Antoine Bourseiller, *Axël* was performed for the first time since 1894 at the Studio des Champs-Elysées on 30 January 1962. Villiers' correspondence was collected and published through the diligent efforts of Joseph Bollery (1962). Finally, *Le Prétendant*, the later version of *Morgane*, was found, published, and performed on French television in 1965.

II *Posthumous Collections*

Chez les passants (1890), published by Mallarmé and Huysmans after Villiers' death, contains seventeen short works, only two of which ("Peintures décoratives," "L'Etonnant Couple Moutonnet") had never appeared before. Ten of these are critical essays,[6] and they are not, it must be admitted, very effective. "Hamlet" (1867) is little more than random thoughts on Shakespeare. "Le Candidat" (1874) and "La Tentation de Saint-Antoine" (1874) are mere homages to Flaubert, while "Une Soirée chez Nina de Villard" (1888) is an homage to poet Léon Dierx, and "Augusta Holmès" (1885) is one to the female musician whom Villiers met at Versailles in 1866. "Souvenir" (1887) praises Wagner for religious conviction, and "Notre-Seigneur Jesus-Christ sur les planches" (1888) is a critique of Rodolphe Darzens' play *L'Amante du Christ*, based on religious, not esthethic, principles. "Lettre sur un livre," written as a preface to Emile Pierre's *Le Rêve d'aimer* (1885), does little more than offer congratulations and encouragement to a fellow author and friend, while "Le Cas extraordinaire de M. Francisque Sarcey" (1887) angrily condemns a theater critic who was unkind to Villiers' *L'Evasion*. The sole piece of art criticism, "Peintures décoratives du foyer de l'Opéra," holds out promise but proves quite disappointing; it ranks far below the quality of art discussions contained in Baudelaire's and Diderot's *Salons*. As Raitt has already suggested, in none of these essays is any attempt made to develop an artistic theory, and none sheds much light on Villiers' own conception of art.[7]

The seven other works in the volume are scarcely more exciting. "Le Socle de la statue" (1882) and "La Couronne présidentielle" (1887) are long, rambling satires about politicians during the Third Republic. "Au Gendre insigne," originally published as part of the latter satire under the title "Le Couronnement de M. Grévy," is equally ponderous. "L'Etonnant Couple Moutonnet" is a macabre tale about a husband and wife whose union is based on their obsession with decapitation. "Le Réalisme dans la peine de mort" (1885), a sort of essay that Villiers himself calls a "few notes . . . jotted down" (*OC*, XI, 127), decries a bourgeois society that has dehumanized death by removing stairs to the guillotine and reducing punishment "to the *strict* necessary" (130). Another polemic essay, "La Suggestion devant la loi" (1888), warns that for justice to be served, officials must make every effort to determine whether an accused has acted freely, for one may well be forced to commit a crime under hypnosis against one's will. Finally, although not without charm, "L'Avertissement" (1883) is more a free association of school-day memories and reflections on the exiled French king than a well-structured story.

A second posthumous collection, *Propos d'Au-delà* (1893), is of considerably greater interest. It joins together three tales that appeared in 1888–1889, three published posthumously between 1890 and 1892, and a fragment from an epistolary novel that was to be written with Judith Gautier. Four of the stories merit attention. The first, entitled "L'Elu des rêves" (1888), is about a poet, Alexis Dufrêne, and his two esthetician friends, J. Bréart and Eusèbe Nédonchel. It pokes fun at critics who dissect and analyze the artist's dream like scientific positivists and who eagerly demonstrate "that it is always necessary to see the things . . . AS THEY ARE" (*OC*, XI, 12). This negative attitude toward theorizing helps to explain why

Villiers left behind such a small number of critical works compared to other writers associated with the Symbolist movement.

"L'Amour sublime" (1889) concerns Evariste Rousseau-Latouche, practical center-left parliamentary representative, who for convenience marries Frédérique d'Allepraine, "a person stricken with soul" (*OC*, XI, 24). Sometime after marriage, Frédérique meets her cousin, who is on a visit to Paris. Like Frédérique, Bénédict d'Allepraine disdains "banal everyday things," possessing a "rather exclusive love of the things above" (28). The two "naturally begin to love each other with an ideal love as chaste as [it was] deep" (29); they talk of the possibility of union in eternity. Evariste naturally feels excluded. Pridefully rejecting a desire to send Bénédict away, the jealous husband sets out to prove that Frédérique and Bénédict "were 'fundamentally' flesh-and-blood beings like him, . . . like 'everybody' " (33). He tempts them, lays traps for them, leaving them alone in the gardens, even feigning departure on business. Nothing works. With their sights on an eternal fulfillment, the chaste lovers are indifferent to carnal pleasure and earthly manifestations of love.

The initial situation of the story recalls a similar one in *La Révolte*, where a "being of the *beyond* [is also] joined to a being of earth" (24). But if Félix (in *La Révolte*) is unwittingly harmful to his wife, Rousseau-Latouche, conceivably named for the philosophe (1712–1778) whose democratic spirit he embodies and the writer (1785–1851) whose antimonarchist feelings he shares, is more like the later Tribulat. Actively cruel, he is determined to destroy a love he does not understand and to reduce to his own categories something that calls in question the neat perimeters of his monolithic world. Villiers does not, however, let the practical spirit triumph. Ironically, Rousseau-Latouche is sadly disappointed because he has not been "deceived" by his wife (36). Hoping to find them in bed at the story's end, he instead finds Frédérique and Bénédict ("the blessed one") innocently leaning over a balcony, looking at the stars. As in "L'Amour suprême," the balcony facing the stars suggests a detachment from earthly concerns and a concentration on eternity.

Another story in the collection, "Le Meilleur Amour" (1889), is also about love and a mismatched couple. One day, the young Breton, Guilhem Kerlis, "whose sentiments were at one and the same time pure, burning, and stable" met a farmer's daughter who was "playful, engaging . . . [but] perhaps a little too laughing" (*OC*, XI, 38). In love with his fantasy, Guilhem does not realize that

Yvaine herself is "incapable of truly solid feelings" (38), while Yvaine, sometimes laughing at Guilhem's ideal and incomprehensible love, would have preferred him "more amusing" (39). When Guilhem leaves for military duty, however, she accepts his ring and promises to wait the five years for him. The wait proves too long. Less than ten months after Guilhem's departure, she yields to a cadet and slides into the life of a "loose woman" (40). Retaining a weakness for Guilhem, whose letters "formed such a contrast with the tone in which the 'others' talked to her" (41), she nonetheless continues to profess in her letters to him unabated fidelity. In the fifth year, while Yvaine is in a hospital bed, suffering from syphilis, Guilhem's letters abruptly stop. She wonders if he has learned about her life and broken their engagement out of shame and grief. The truth is that he has been wounded in action and has died happy, believing Yvaine chaste and faithful.

The title of the story, "The Best Love," is by no means ironic. In keeping with illusionistic philosophy, and as demonstrated in *Akëdyssëril* and *L'Eve future*, Villiers believed that all love is illusionary, that one necessarily falls in love with a mental construct, and that the maintenance of love depends on the maintenance of illusion. Guilhem imagines Yvaine ideal, chastely loves that dream, and thinks their love perfect. The ideal Yvaine and perfect love thus actually exist for him, since he believes in them and since his illusions are not interrupted by reality. To be sure, Guilhem "was born under a happy star, and . . . few men were more favored in their love than he" (37). His fate would have been far different if he had returned from service to marry Yvaine. After a brief moment of ecstasy, powerless to maintain his illusion in the face of reality, he would have realized "the trifling, lazy, inconsistent, coquettish, and dangerous nature of his wife" (42). Love would have vanished, and he would have lived out a "formidable old age" in misery (43). The ironic thing about the story is the wide discrepancy between dream and reality and the fact that Guilhem's blissful ending comes at the very moment Yvaine is suffering a syphilitic death.

The final tale in the collection worth noting is "Les Filles de Milton" (1891), set after the restoration of the British monarchy (1660), in the first years of Charles II's reign (1660–1685). The ex-foreign secretary of Cromwell's Commonwealth government (1649–1655), now poor and blind, is living in seclusion. His days are devoted to writing *Paradise Lost* (1658–1665), which his daughters transcribe under his dictation. As the tale opens, Deborah Milton is engaged in conversation with her mother. She expresses hope God will recall her father, no longer useful to anybody (*OC*, XI, 45), complains that noblemen will not marry the daughters of an "old rhymester without bread, who voted for his king's death" (46), and assails Milton's poetry as an "unbearable jingle of empty words" (46). Despite her mother's reprimands, she then complains of hunger and the old man's obsession with *Paradise Lost*, which he imagines "will dominate memories in Posterity" (47). At length, she reiterates her hope that Milton will die, for they could then "change names, go abroad, [and] live" (47). After this harangue, she leaves to borrow money. Emma, the other daughter, returns carrying firewood, soon followed by Deborah, who has only obtained two shillings.

Milton in Puritan dress now enters. He orders his daughters to write legibly and, above all, to transcribe his words faithfully. Although realizing that his words will go unappreciated by a world that "only prizes the void" (50), he knows that he is "among the so-called poets . . . a living among the dead" (50) and that his thought will live on after him. Deborah, doubting he has enough common sense to write, asks whether he should not be resting in bed. The "seer of divine things" (52) defiantly claims that his words contain the breath of God and begins to recite one of the most beautiful passages in *Paradise Lost*, indeed in all the English language: "Hail, holy Light, offspring of Heav'n first-born . . ."[8] Deborah and Emma ask him to start again, as he has dictated too fast. It is too late; he has already forgotten what he has said.

Despite the research Villiers performed at the Bibliothèque Nationale,[9] it is clear that the author intended this tale to be more than a simple recounting of history and that he unhesitantly transformed the facts to underline the symbolic significance of the story. Physically blind, sensitive only to eternal truths, forgotten by the world, the historical Milton is almost a natural symbol of the seer rejected by society. But to make the symbol of all the more poignant, Villiers describes Milton as poor and hungry, which is a slight exaggeration of historical truth. Moreover, despite a prevailing legend of friction within the Milton household, it is far from sure that Milton's grown daughters, in fact numbering three, Deborah, Mary, and the crippled Anne, actually resented their father or misesteemed his verse. Yet Villiers adopts the legend, embroiders upon it, and paints the daughters as valuing their material comfort more than the poet's verse and as totally ignorant of the poetic process—Deborah makes that clear when she asks if Milton has the necessary *common sense* to write (51). In his hands, then, the two daughters become symbols of a bourgeois society that ridicules the poet and utterly rejects the wisdom of his words.

Unfortunately, the tale as we have it is only a sketch of what it was to be. The rough areas in the middle, such as the daughters' frantic comings and goings and Emma's unexplained return, make that apparent. Yet, in spite of its unfinished state, "Les Filles de Milton" is one of Villiers' most beautiful tales. This is not just because of its symbolism and the animated dialogue. Few other stories by Villiers convey the depth of feeling expressed here. Quite obviously, the author sympathized with the blind poet and viewed himself as a modern-day Milton, at odds with the society in which he lived.

II Axël

The history of this drama is curious and, owing to lack of documentation, not totally clear. It was conceived early in Villiers' career,[10] and writing probably began around 1870. At least a first act was complete by 1872, for it appeared on 12 October of that year in the *Renaissance littéraire et artistique*. After that, Villiers probably gave up work on the play; when he returned to it, sometime after 1880, it was probably no longer with the intention of producing it.[11] Surely the failure of *La Révolte* and troubles with *Le Nouveau Monde* had persuaded him that no play of his could succeed on stage as long as the public's taste remained as it was. Still he continued writing, hoping that someday conditions would change. A first version was published in *La Jeune France* between November 1885 and June 1886, although it may have been virtually complete as early as February 1884, when Villiers delivered readings from the work before a group of his enthusiasts (*Corr*, II, 55–57). After publication, the first version was retouched and, despite Villiers' announcement in 1889 that the revision was definitive and ready to print, it did not appear (*Corr*, II, 263–65; *OC*, IV, 273). At his death the galleys of the second version were still being proofed. It was left for Mallarmé and Huysmans to publish the manuscript a year later.

Part One, entitled "The Religious World," takes place on Christmas Eve around 1828 in the chapel of a pseudo-Catholic convent in Flanders. To save an endangered soul as well as to enrich the order,

the Abbess has decided that her beautiful, intelligent but sullen
ward, Princess Sara de Maupers, will pronounce her religious vows
at midnight. Sara has already shown herself unwilling, but the nun
hopes that confinement and privation have worn away resistance.
Before the ceremony, the Abbess cautions the officiating Archdeacon that Sara is prideful, has studied works of an occult Rosi-
crucian sect that occupied the convent three centuries ago, and has
probably deciphered some occult clue in a parchment sent there by
a Master Janus. The Archdeacon is confident that he can cure Sara's
indecision with his homily of exhortation. During the ceremony,
however, when he asks Sara if she accepts Light, Hope, and Life,
she breaks her silence with a resounding "No" (*OC*, IV, 46). Not
seeing what has happened, the nuns in the choir continue their
hymn of jubilation until the angered Abbess silences them and
sends them scurrying. The Archdeacon then tries to punish Sara for
her sacrilege by locking her in an *in-pace*. But Sara seizes an axe
from among the ex-voto offerings and forces the priest into the
prison. Closing the slab, she flees the cloister to search for the gold
she has read about in the parchment.

The rest of the drama takes place in the medieval fortress of the
Auërsperg family, deep in the German Black Forest. It is now Easter Eve. As Part Two, "The Tragic World," begins, Miklaus,
Hartwig, and Gotthold, three veteran soldiers, are discussing their
lord, Count Axël of Auërsberg, his occult mentor, Master Janus, and
a visiting cousin, Commander Kaspar of Auërsperg. The three retainers and Axël's page Ukko withdraw as the Commander enters.
In a soliloquy, the latter, the epitome of materialistic, bourgeois
values, admits wanting Axël to leave his solitary existence devoted
to occultism to assume a position in the world, where "he would
become a most useful instrument" (92). Now, fearful he will die with
an awesome secret, Herr Zacharias the steward reveals to Kaspar
that three hundred fifty million thalers, transported south for
safekeeping during the Napoleonic war under the direction of Axël's
now-deceased father, are buried somewhere in the caverns near the
fortress. Overcome by desire for the gold, the Commander plots to
kill his cousin after questioning him about its location (of which Axël
is ignorant). When indirection reveals nothing, Kaspar asks directly
about the treasure. Out of hospitality Axël has for too long tolerated
his cousin's materialistic values, but the latter has now unforgivably
"made use of [his] leisure here . . . [,] uncovered one of the most

important secrets of [the] house" (147), and even plotted against his host. In order that the gold remain a secret, he not be tempted by it, and his retreat remain forever unravaged by excavators, Axël provokes the commander into a duel and kills him.

At the beginning of Part Three, called "The Occult World," Axël tells his preceptor that the Commander has mysteriously reawakened in him dead desires, turned his mind from occult studies, and "called [him] back to earth" and thoughts of gold (189–90). Janus urges Axël to continue to become "an intelligence freed from the . . . bonds of the moment" (198) and to cast off the world's veils. But the magus's words are to no avail. When he asks his student if he accepts Light, Hope, and Life, Axël, like Sara before him, responds with a resounding "No" (213). For love of gold, he rejects the occult asceticism he once cherished. Gotthold then announces that a woman is waiting. With a mysterious winter-blooming rose on the cross of her dagger, emblem of the Rosicrucians, Sara has at last reached the fortress. In an aside, Master Janus announces that his work is about to be accomplished (216).

The final part, "The World of Passion," takes place in the gallery of tombs in the underground vaults of the Auërsperg fortress. The military retainers, Herr Zacharias, and Ukko have just buried the Commander when Axël, who has realized the world's vanity and decided on suicide (226), arrives to bid his comrades farewell. No sooner do the latter depart than Sara enters. Pressing a sword blade on a heraldic death's-head, she opens a wall and discloses dark galleries that extend to the depths of the subterranean caverns. Gems and gold shower down from the opening and envelop her. Sensing Axël's presence, wanting to safeguard the treasure, she turns and twice fires a pistol at him. Although wounded, Axël overcomes his assailant, wrenches a knife from her hand, and turns it on her. Axël's animosity is at once turned to passion when he sees the woman's beauty. Sara too is overwhelmed by feeling. "I know nothing but you," she says to Axël, "I date only from an hour ago: what preceded that hour is no longer" (242). They seem to have everything: love, power, wealth; Sara wants to fly to the farthest corners of the world to fulfill all their dreams (259). But now Axël cautions: "Our existence is [already] full,—and its cup runneth over!" (261). He knows that they have just experienced an ideal moment of love that can only pale hereafter. He therefore persuades Sara to flee the world with him and preserve forever that moment of happiness. As a chorus of woodcutters and Ukko's greeting to his wife sound in the background, the lovers drink poison and die in each other's arms, "exchanging on the lips the supreme sigh" (270). The light of Easter dawn filters through a window; the distant murmur of the wind can be heard.

What message did Villiers wish to convey by this complex drama? We recall first that in Part One Sara renounces Christian asceticism in favor of worldly gold. In Part Two, Axël rejects the materialistic life of the Commander, while in Part Three he succumbs to the temptation of gold and repudiates the occult asceticism he has long espoused. Finally, in Part Four, both Axël and Sara realize the vanity of the gold they have sought as well as the earthly love they have discovered, outrightly reject a life based on them, and opt for death through suicide. Disdainfully, Axël remarks: "Live? The servants will do that for us" (261). Viewed in this way, the drama clearly presents four symbolic approaches to life—religious commitment, materialistic pleasure, nonreligious asceticism, and earthly love and power. One by one, the protagonists demonstrate the insufficiency and worthlessness of these possibilities. One is led to the inexorable conclusion that the author was trying to convince us that all approaches to life are inane, life itself is inane, and the only rational recourse is the one taken by his protagonists: complete rejection of life and escape into infinity through suicide. Villiers' message, in one critic's words, constitutes nothing less than a new religion, an "anti-Gospel, Gospel of Death, in opposition to the [Christian] Gospel of Life."[12]

A close analysis of the drama leaves little doubt that Villiers was proposing this pessimistic abandonment of the world as a new cult and the play's protagonists as new Christs, Messiahs of that new religion. Emmanuèle, the name given to Sara (14), recalls the name given to the Christian savior (Isaiah 7:14; 8:8), while the x, so prominent in Axël's name (borrowed perhaps from contemporary novels or Scandinavian legend[13]), is the symbol of Christ himself. The protagonists' lives even parallel the Christian Messiah's. As the Son's destiny was ordained by the Father, theirs has been by Janus. This magus, who functions both as Axël's tutor and the force shaping destiny, selects the aristocratic Maupers and Auërsperg houses to bear the chosen two (OC, IV, 20), arranges a meeting between them (190, 216), entices Sara from the convent by sending a clue about the lost gold (24) and foreordains Axël's rejection of occultism so that he might rise to greater glory (190, 216). Moreover, as Christ was born into the world on Christmas, Sara is born into worldly awareness and desire on the same day. In the period after Christmas, Sara and Axël, like Christ, undergo a period of trial and temptation, their own Lent. Like the Son, who rejected the devil's temptations and the Pharisees' taunts, the protagonists succeed in overcoming the temptations of Christianity, materialism, occultism, and love/gold as well as rebuffing the criticism of priest and seer. Finally, Axël's and Sara's destiny is accomplished and the meaning of the mottos highlighting their names—"Macte Animo! Ultima PERfulget Sola"; "AltiUs rEsurgeRe SPERo Gemmatus"[14]—fulfilled when they accept death and entry into infinity on Easter, the very day of Christ's resurrection and fulfillment of destiny.

Not only do the names and lives of the protagonists resemble Christ's, so does their mission. By their deaths they too found and consecrate a new religion. Moreover, their lives, like Christ's, are to serve as an ideal and model for all mankind. Axël makes this clear when just before he dies he expresses this hope: "May the human race, free of its vain chimeras, vain despairs, all the lies that dazzle eyes made to grow dim—consenting no longer to play this bleak enigma—yes, may the race end, fleeing unconcerned like us, without even bidding you, old earth, farewell" (270).

One may well wonder what caused Villiers' advocacy of a suicide cult toward the end of his life. Far from shocking, this stance seems an almost inevitable consequence of the illusionistic philosophy that he created and that came to dominate his thinking around 1880. If everything is illusion and nothing has reality unless one confers it through belief, then Villiers must have realized that one system of thought has as much validity as any other.[15] Christianity has as much worth as Hegelianism, and this in turn is as valid as occultism. Pushed to the extreme, then, illusionistic theory made belief in any system impossible, since it justified all systems and at the same time rendered them all equally uncertain. Belief in love or gold and the promises they held out came to be equally impossible for Villiers. In keeping with illusionism, love (as already showed in *Akëdysséril* and *L'Eve future*) as well as happiness based on gold were necessarily illusions, concepts of the imagination. Reality could never equal these imagined dreams but only destroy them. The sole way to preserve love and happiness was to flee life before reality intervened and to affix them in eternity through death. Removing the prospect of any belief or happiness on earth, Villiers' illusionism could lead only to voluntary death.

Now, if this atheistic nihilism does constitute the correct reading of the play, how can we explain the words, "breaking the silence of the dreadful place where two human beings, by their own choice, have just consecrated their souls to the exile of HEAVEN" (271), at the end of the 1886 and 1890 editions? The line is problematic since it outrightly condemns the suicide of the lovers and thus throws into question Villiers' supposed espousal of nihilism. In seeking an explanation, one recalls that the greater part of the play was complete by 1885. Yet, around that time, Villiers experienced a revival of his Catholic faith. The reordained believer must have been troubled and embarrassed by the strong anti-Christian message of *Axël*. No doubt, then, he added this line in a feeble attempt to assuage his conscience and counteract the play's iconoclastic effect. This interpretation seems plausible for two reasons. First, as we have already noted, Villiers reacted similarly to *L'Eve future*. Bothered by its anti-Christian sentiment, he added a final chapter around 1885 to bring the novel into conformity with his refound orthodoxy. Second, we know that after Villiers published *Axël*, he contemplated extensive revisions. Huysmans claims that one quarter of the third act as well as the fourth, where "the cross would intervene," were to be completely revamped (273–74). And Remy de Gourmont supports this claim when he writes that at the end of the play "the Cross was to appear, condeming the act" of suicide.[16] Fragments outlining a proposed Christian dénouement have actually come down to us (275–83). Surely Villiers sensed that the addition of one line to the 1886 play could hardly undo the pessimistic import of all that preceded and that greater revisions would be necessary.

The fact that Villiers never did adopt these revisions certainly suggests that he was dissatisfied with them and rightly saw they rendered the play as a whole incoherent.[17] Yet his hesitancy to republish the play with the original ending, witnessed by his holding on to proofs, all the while claiming that the work was finished, suggests that he still objected to the drama on moral grounds. Villiers must have been torn between publishing an artistically satisfying work that ignored his renewed faith and publishing an artistically incoherent one that demonstrated his religious conviction. Death cruelly intervened, and Villiers never succeeded in charting a safe course between Scylla and Charybdis.

Having studied the play's meaning, let us look at some formal considerations. The first is structure. Although divided into four parts, the play really seems to have been conceived as three, each with similar themes.[18] The first division (Part One) concerns Sara and introduces the themes of tantalizing gold and renunciation, in this case a renunciation of monastic Christianity. The second division (Parts Two and Three) tells Axël's story. It resounds the renunciation theme, in varied form, however, for here it is a question of Axël's repudiation of the material world; reintroduces the theme of the alluring gold, as the Commander's desires are passed on to Axël; then reinvokes the theme of renunciation, when the latter rejects occult asceticism to pursue the gold. One notices that the temptation and renunciation of Axël parallel those of Sara earlier. The final segment (Part Four) brings the first two together, for it deals with both renunciators, who meet and fall in love, and intertwines the gold and renunciation themes, distinct up to now. Here, in addition to the temptation of love, the lovers renounce the gold that has long exercised dominion over them.

The characters in the play are far removed from everyday life. They move in a legendary world of shadow, darkness, and medieval arches, where, despite the announced time of 1828, the spirit of the nineteenth century has not yet penetrated.[19] Frequently, like Sara in the first part, they scarcely move but assume posed positions (10, 14, 45, 46, 64, 114, 134, 140, 146, 151, 184–85, 214, 226, 240, 271). If they move, it is in slow stately fashion (32–33, 48–49, 56, 65, 182, 195, 213, 216, 228–30). They deliver declarations, long even for the theater, let alone life (51–56, 155–64, 170–80, 205–208, 251–56). Their language is lyrical, rich in imagery, and quite unlike everyday speech. Moreover, the characters display little of the intricacy and frailty of human psychology. Sara and Axël, for example, incarnate an ideal humanity with superhuman beauty, intelligence, personality, and determination. The mesmerizing effect Sara has on Sister Aloyse (17–18, 28–29) is one indication of that dynamic force, while the renunciation of love and gold by Sara and Axël is the final proof of superiority. The secondary characters, on the other hand, are outright embodiments of spiritual forces. The Abbess and Archdeacon, for instance, represent a religious ideal, whereas Janus the tutor embodies occult asceticism. The character of the Commander, who at one point says "I call myself *real life*" (128), clearly symbolizes a materialistic ideal. Finally, the characters seem removed from life, since everything they do and everything that touches them has symbolic import. Axël's duel with the Commander graphically suggests an antagonism between ideal humanity and materialism; the slaying of the latter symbolizes Axël's momentary triumph over the world. The howling winds that surround Auërsberg's castle are symbolic of the world trying to engulf the retreat (271). Axël's arm-crossing and prolonged stare following his renunciation of Janus (214) suggest his stubbornness and steadfastness of decision. Lastly, the entrance of Axël and Sara into the tomb at the beginning of Part Four is symbolic of their forthcoming death.

In spite of the solemnity surrounding the characters, the play contains moments of comedy that approach sheer buffoonery. One example is the unsuccessful attempt by the Abbess to silence the hymn of jubilation after Sara has refused to take the veil and effectively removed all reason for the convent to rejoice (47–48). A second instance comes in Part Two, where an enthusiastic Ukko longs to tell Miklaus, Hartwig, and Gotthold the news of his forthcoming marriage but is constantly thwarted by the retainers' paternal fussing and puerile interruption (79–82). Finally, there is a bit of comedy in the burial scene at the beginning of Part Four (220–23). Here the youthful, loose-tongued Ukko shows little respect for the dead Commander and is constantly silenced by the old retainers, who call him "a nursling with milk still on [his] nose" (222) and who pride themselves on their sense of decorum.

Doubtlessly, there is some similarity between this play's setting and that of Victor Hugo's *Les Burgraves* (1843) and *Torquémada* (1882). No doubt too Axël somewhat resembles the main character of Goethe's *Faust*.[20] But the foregoing discussion makes the drama's affinities with Wagnerian opera clear and unmistakable. Its structure, not unlike parallel movements in music, containing thematic variations, followed by a synthesizing coda; its solemn, statuesque, symbolic characters that deliver lyrical passages resembling arias; and the comic intermezzi involving the secondary characters recall elements in the German's works. When one takes into account the incidental music in the play (82, 113), the embryonic system of musical leitmotifs that Villiers may have chosen to develop (247), and the choruses that comment upon the dramatic action (32, 33–35, 42–44, 47–48, 257–58, 269), one realizes that the influence of Wagner on Villiers was pervasive. The similarity between the theme of gold in *Axël* and *Das Ring*, as well as between the lovers' suicide and the *liebestod* in *Tristan und Isolde*, only serves to make that influence more apparent. One is necessarily led to conclude that Villiers was again attempting his own *Gesamtkunstwerk*, in obvious imitation of Wagner, as he already had with *Le Nouveau Monde*.

The play has been criticized for its relative lack of action, its stylized characters, and its unexplained turns of events, such as Axël's abrupt conversion from occultism to worldly desire in Part Three.[21] One has to admit that these criticisms would be well-founded if Villiers had intended a play mirroring life as he had attempted in *La Révolte* and *Le Prétendant*. In dramas with realistic and historic frameworks, one has every right to expect characters to move like humans, act consistently if not logically, and reveal a subtle psychology that characterizes most of the human race. Yet, it must be clear by now that here Villiers had no such intention. Quite the contrary. He set out to create an idealistic play that would be in total contrast to the realistic-naturalistic drama, the "well-made play" then in vogue. This new drama endeavored to create an aura of mystery. Its orientation was less psychological than philosophic and symbolic. It was little concerned with external action; through a highly poeticized language freed from the bonds of rhetoric, it was to evoke the ultimate essence of souls. Music and other arts were aids in evoking these moods.

No doubt *Axël* can be criticized. The philosophy Janus exposes in Part Three can hardly be understood by anyone not initiated into those ancient rites. The development of Parts Two and Three weighs down the play and obscures its original tripartite structure. Janus' dual function as tutor and overseer of destiny is sometimes confusing. But it is utter injustice to fault the play for want of action, for stylized characters, or for psychologically unexplained events. Such criticism bespeaks a misunderstanding of the author's goal in undertaking the drama.

Clearly, *Axël* holds a special place among Villiers' writings. In his preface to *La Révolte*, published in 1870, just after returning from Germany, Villiers called for reform of the French stage. For close to twenty years, he labored in hopes of bringing that dream to reality. *Axël* remains the last and clearest example of his efforts to imitate Wagnerian opera, to transplant qualities of it to France, and in so doing, to revivify the flagging Gallic theater. The drama is unique for another reason. Works like *Isis* and "Claire Lenoir" demonstrate

Villiers' early philosophical gropings while later works, like *L'Eve future* and some stories, reveal snatches of his emerging illusionistic ideas. *Axël* alone expounds *in extenso* the attitudes toward life that Villiers reached in later years. The drama unfavorably describes forms of philosophy he once espoused, follows his developing illusionistic theories to their logical conclusions, and gives the "final expression to his peculiar idealism."[22] Summa or synthesis seems an appropriate word to describe *Axël*: It not only brings to fruition twenty years of dreams concerning the theater, it also synthesizes as many years of philosophical reflection. Villiers' preoccupation with the play throughout his career, as well as the numerous revisions he made upon it, right up to the moment of his death, suggest that he fully intended it as some final statement of his life and work. If then Villiers had a life work, *Axël* was certainly it.

Conclusion

DESPITE apparent diversity, Villiers' work has an underlying unity. The form may be lyric, dramatic, or narrative; the theme occult, Hegelian, or illusionistic; the tone serious or satiric; but everything Villiers wrote, from *Premières Poésies* to *Axël*, has the character of an idealistic crusade against the materialistic forces of his age. Living in a society he despised, a society committed to money, positivism, scientific progress, and democratic mediocrity, this modern, lay Augustine denounced the world, placed his faith in an embattled, coterminous world of the spirit—the inner life of man (*En dedans*) and the eternal, impersonal beyond (*Au-delà*)[1]—and dedicated himself to its defense. Pieces like "La Machine à gloire" and "Les Demoiselles de Bienfilâtre" ridicule a materialistic world where mediocre men, devoid of spiritual dimension, subvert human values. Others, like "L'Inconnue," *Isis, Elën, La Révolte*, and *Le Prétendant*, portray the beauty of the spiritual realm, while *L'Eve future* attempts to prove its very existence. And his last work, *Axël*, advocates fleeing the world to attain the other one in all its plentitude.

George Moore (1852–1933), Irish novelist and frequenter of Parisian salons in his youth, once remarked that Villiers as writer was a failure (*raté*).[2] If he meant that Villiers failed to gain widespread popularity during life and after death, then he was right, although one might well question his definition of success. After all, Stendhal was virtually unknown during his lifetime, Diderot acquired recognition only years after death, and Virginia Woolf does not and maybe never will have a large following. On the other hand, if he meant that Villiers' work was of little consequence and little artistic merit, then he was clearly wrong and his judgment betrays an acute myopia.

143

Critics before us have already demonstrated the important role that Villiers played in the formation of the Symbolist movement and his legacy to later writers.[3] Not only did he hand down a whole series of images (the aloof woman, the seer, artist-swans), but more fundamentally, he disseminated notions of German idealism, the metaphysical basis of Symbolism, and by his profession of faith in mystery and the spirit, encouraged the Symbolists and those who followed "to turn their backs on reality" for a world of dreams.[4] Equally important, he helped popularize the music of Wagner, an incontestable idol of the movement, and his *Axël*, modeled on Wagnerian opera, marked the beginning of Symbolist theater.[5] This tradition would be carried on by Maurice Maeterlinck (1862–1949), Paul Claudel (1868–1955), and W. B. Yeats (1865–1939).

Furthermore, we have demonstrated in this study the artistic merit of Villiers' work. It is true that much of his poetry is derivative and bombastic, that his criticism is uninteresting—Any critical sense he had was "absorbed in himself . . . [and] the creative process"[6]—and that he is not at ease in narrative works of long duration. Although imaginative and colorful, both *Isis* and *L'Eve future* are marred by descriptive digressions that slow action and tire the reader. On the other hand, his dramas, by which he hoped to achieve renown, display greater talent. *Le Prétendant*, the best of his realistic-historic plays, is compelling theater despite melodramatic touches, while *Le Nouveau Monde* and *Axël* are ingenious attempts to combine drama with symbols, music, and other art forms. Ironically, in a life full of ironies, his tales, a genre Villiers esteemed less than the theater—"Bah! anecdotes!" he supposedly said[7]—display his greatest talents. The best of them—his first three, most of the *Contes cruels*, a dozen or so in *L'Amour suprême*, *Histoires insolites*, *Nouveaux Contes cruels*, and *Propos d'Au-delà*—are masterpieces, "crystals perfect in shape, pure in color, and endless in variety."[8] As concentrated as Mérimée's, as varied as Maupassant's, as magnetic as Edgar Allan Poe's, these short stories are some of the best ever written.

Villiers de l'Isle-Adam may not be a Diderot, Stendhal, or Virginia Woolf; his work lacks the sweep, human understanding, and esthetic consistency of theirs. But he is hardly the failure Moore claimed. By his influence and the brilliance of his dramas and stories, he figures among the most important writers of the nineteenth century. The English-speaking world has refused him recognition, indeed any recognition, for too long. Certainly he deserves more than the tomb of neglect where we have buried him. "Lazarus, come forth!"

Abbreviations

OC   Villiers de l'Isle-Adam. *Oeuvres complètes.* Paris: Mercure de France, 1914–1931. 11 vols.

Corr   Villiers de l'Isle-Adam. *Correspondance générale et documents inédits,* ed., Joseph Bollery. Paris: Mercure de France, 1962. 2 vols.

CC   Villiers de l'Isle-Adam. *Contes cruels, Nouveaux Contes cruels,* ed., Pierre-Georges Castex. Paris: Garnier, 1968.

Droug   Villiers de l'Isle-Adam. *Les Trois Premiers Contes,* ed., E. Drougard. Paris: Les Belles Lettres, 1931. 2 vols.

LP   Villiers de l'Isle-Adam. *Le Prétendant,* ed., P.-G. Castex and A. W. Raitt. Paris: José Corti, 1965.

Notes and References

Preface

1. Denis Diderot, *Le Neveu de Rameau* in *Oeuvres* (Paris: Bibliothèque de la Pléiade, 1951), p. 469.

Chapter One

1. See, for example, Mme de Carfort's letter to her sister, 10 March 1846 (*Corr*, I, 23). See also her letter of 16 March 1846 to the same person (*Corr*, I, 25).
2. See article 8 of the marriage contract between the marquis and Mlle de Carfort, reprinted by Gustave Guiches in "Villiers de l'Isle-Adam: documents inédits," *La Nouvelle Revue*, 64 (1890), 92.
3. "Lasciate ogni speranza," *Premières Poésies, OC*, X, 142.
4. In primary schools, "reading, writing, elements of French and arithmetic, legal system of weights and measures, religious and moral instruction" were taught. See P. Chevallier, *L'Enseignement français de la Révolution à nos jours* (Paris: Mouton, 1968), p. 71. On secondary schools, their programs, and their stress on French and Latin composition, see Antoine Prost, *Histoire de l'enseignement en France 1800–1967* (Paris: Colin, 1968), pp. 48–56.
5. Louis Tiercelin, "Villiers de l'Isle-Adam," *La Nouvelle Revue*, 6 (1900), 36.
6. Robert du Pontavice de Heussey; *Villiers de l'Isle-Adam: His Life and Works*, tr. Mary Loyd (New York: Dodd, Mead, 1894), p. 24. The biographer is the son of Hyacinthe du Pontavice de Heussey, a distant cousin of Villiers, at whose house he may have met Baudelaire. Robert reports (not always reliably) much on his father's testimony, although he himself knew Villiers.
7. See Prost, pp. 50–51.
8. On Villiers' Latin, see, for example, his verson of "cette souveraine devise des grands artistes: *Unus amor, unus ars*" (*OC*, XI, 113), which contains an error most diligent schoolboys would avoid. In the letter to

Catulle Mendès, the passage in Latin contains numerous errors, among which are: *obliviscere*, instead of the deponent infinitive *oblivisci; de nigros* for *de nigris; ideirco* for *idcirco; sine sumnos* for *sine somnis; mansus sum*, a Gallicized Latin for *mansi;* and *possa fuit* for *potuerat.*

9. Account of Count H. Le Noir de Tournemine, cited by E. de Rougemont, *Villiers de l'Isle-Adam* (Paris: Mercure de France, 1910), pp. 54–55.

10. Tiercelin, p. 36. Pontavice (pp. 26, 33) cites only one romance.

11. Cf. Pontavice, pp. 26, 33; *Contes et récits*, ed., Jacques Chupeau (Paris: Bordas, 1970), p. 5; *CC*, introduction, p. iv.

12. Cf. Rougemont, p. 63.

13. Tiercelin, p. 36.

14. *Ibid.*, p. 38.

15. See *ibid.*, p. 43.

16. Tiercelin, p. 39.

17. Drougard, "L' 'Axël' de Villiers de l'Isle-Adam," *Revue d'Histoire Litteraire de la France*, 42 (1935), 511.

18. Tiercelin, p. 42.

19. Cf. Pontavice, pp. 35–45; Chupeau, p. 7; *CC*, introduction, p. iv. Others claim Villiers' family came with him earlier (Cf. *Corr*, I, 15; Rougemont, pp. 61–62).

20. Pontavice, p. 35.

21. Concerning Le Menant and Villiers, see Tiercelin, p. 45. After 1859 there were only infrequent contacts. Villiers sought prayers for his dead great-aunt from Amédée Le Menant (*Corr*, I, 171) and congratulated him on the publication of a book (*Corr*, II, 239). As for Lemercier de Neuville, consult his *Souvenirs d'un montreur de marionnettes* (Paris: Bauche, 1911), pp. 90–92.

22. A. W. Raitt, *Villiers de l'Isle-Adam et le mouvement symboliste* (Paris: José Corti, 1965), p. 14.

23. Droug, I, 9. See Also *Corr*, I, 47.

24. A proposed volume of verse, *Les Assomptions*, never appeared (*Corr*, I, 41). But "Chemin de fer" appeared in *Le Publicateur des Côtes-du-Nord*, 12 September 1863; revised, it was printed in *Le Parnasse contemporain*, 1866, as "Esquisse à la manière de Goya." Other examples of his later poetry include "Hélène," "A une grande forêt," and "A une enfant taciturne," which also appeared in the latter journal. Moreover, Villiers composed a poem for *Isis*, and a series of poems, among them "Hélène," was included in *Contes cruels* (1883). See *CC*, pp. 474–81.

25. On *La Causerie*, see Lemercier de Neuville, p. 103; on its editor, Victor Cochinat, see *ibid.*, pp. 60–62.

26. Rougemont, p. 72; Victor-Emile Michelet, *Villiers de l'Isle-Adam* (Paris: Durville, 1910), p. 45; Verlaine, "Vingt-sept biographies," in

Oeuvres complètes (Paris: Messein, 1949), V, 306; other generalizations in Max Daireaux, *Villiers de l'Isle-Adam* (Paris: Desclée de Brouwer, 1936), pp. 34, 273.

27. See Daireaux, p. 273.

28. See Dina Lanfredini, *Villiers de l'Isle-Adam* (Florence: Felice Le Monnier, 1940), p. 11, n. 1.

29. Villiers quoted from memory imprecisely. He has: "Il en est un plus beau, plus grand, plus poétique, / Que personne n'a fait" (*OC*, X, 57). Musset's text reads: "Il en est un plus grand, plus beau, plus poétique, / Que personne n'a fait" (xxiv).

30. Léon-François Hoffmann, *Romantique Espagne* (Princeton: Princeton University Press, 1961), p. 41.

31. Daireaux, p. 273.

32. "My soul is like the crags, whose summits / Seeing the waves flee, bend their bare caverns / Over their own chasms." The title to this poem, incidentally, is from Dante (*Inferno*, III, 9).

33. Then, awakening! death! changing existence!
O Time! icy old man! what have you done with my angel?
Where have you put her, alas! cold, fore'er amiss?
What have you done with the young child full of charms,
What have you done with the smile, what have you done with the tears,
Oh! what have you done with our bliss?

34. Peace of our childhood home! honor, treasure so frail!
Power, vacillating on a throne of shale!
Prayer, humble bliss! glory, pleasure high!
You, knowledge, word full of unfathomable vanity!
These are the futilities of our wretched destiny:
Our only goal is to die!

35. "Weak," i.e., a rhyme where one syllable echoes the other ("arcades," "balustrades"), is opposed to "adequate," i.e., a rhyme where final vowels are supported by identical consonants ("bordés," "dés"), and "rich," i.e., a rhyme where each word has two sounds of equal value ("funèbres," "tenèbres").

36. "You stop, seeking which route followed / Your small boat in the blue furrow"; "To the sounds of the sacred hymn / That sang under the great expanse of bare sky / Everything scarcely created / To its unknown Creator."

37. Miguel de Unamuno, *Poesías*, in *Obras completas* (Madrid: Escelicer, 1966–1970), VI, 298–303.

38. In truth, the epigraph to Canto I is virtually a copy of Isaiah 64: 10, and part of verse 11; "ecce" has been added and "nostrae" has been changed twice to "tuae" in Villiers' version. The epigraph to Canto II is drawn from Isaiah 64:5–7: "peccavimus" from verse 5, most of verse 6 intact, and the second half of verse 7. In the third epigraph, "Vide, Domine, afflictionem populi tui" is modeled on Exodus 3:7 or Lamentations 1:9; "mitte quem

missurus es" reproduces exactly Exodus 4:13, and "Emitte Agnum . . .
Sion," Isaiah 16:1; the last clause "ut auferat, ipse, jugum captivitatis nostrae" is perhaps modeled on Exodus 8:8, Exodus 10:17, Isaiah 14:25, Isaiah
27:9, or I Macabees 8:18. Rather than mislabeling these verses out of
carelessness or lapse of memory, it seems more likely that Villiers purposely
attributed them to the Book of Psalms, perhaps because of this book's
celebrated poetic quality.

    39. Martin Nozick, *Miguel de Unamuno* (New York: Twayne, 1971),
p. 168. The poem "Barcarolle," for example, carries the postscript "Golfe
de Gênes, mars 185 . . ."; it is extremely unlikely that Villiers visited
Genoa. Moreover, in "Exil," the poet bemoans his leaving his supposed
native lands of Ischia and the Antilles.

Chapter Two

    1. *Le Boulevard*, 31 August 1862.
    2. Daireaux, p. 65; Drougard, Introduction to *Les Trois Premiers
Contes*, I, 9; Raitt, p. 88. The latter (p. 226) also suggests another theory:
Perhaps it was Villiers' inability to synthesize Hegelianism and Christianity
that made him abandon the novel.
    3. Pontavice, pp. 70–82.
    4. Raitt, p. 267. See Georges Jean-Aubry, *Une Amitié exemplaire* (Paris:
Mercure de France, 1942).
    5. See *Corr*, I, 74, commentary.
    6. Rougemont, pp. 112–18.
    7. Daireaux, pp. 88, 92. Villiers' bitterness is evident in a letter to
Mallarmé (*Corr*, I, 111–12), written a little later, 27 September 1867.
    8. See *Corr*, I, 102; Mallarmé, *Villiers de l'Isle-Adam* (Brussels:
Lacomblez, 1892), p. 30; Raitt, pp. 14–16.
    9. Raitt, pp. 154–55.
    10. *La Lune*, 18 August 1867.
    11. See Raitt, pp. 53, 55, 87–88, 100.
    12. Daireaux, p. 97.
    13. George Moore, *Memoirs of My Dead Life* (New York: Appleton,
1907), p. 77; Maria Deenen, *Le Merveilleux dans l'oeuvre de Villiers de
l'Isle-Adam* (Paris: Courville, 1939), p. 118; Daireaux, p. 97.
    14. Raitt, pp. 102–104.
    15. "L'Exposition internationale de Peinture de Munich en 1869," *Le
Rappel*, 21 August 1869, reprinted in *Nouvelles littéraires*, 29 July 1939.
    16. Raitt, p. 109. It is possible that Villiers attended the French pre-
miere of Wagner's *Lohengrin* in Brussels on 22 March 1870. Raitt claims he
did (p. 113); other critics are less sure.
    17. *Le Constitutionnel*, 1 August 1870, reprinted in *Nouvelles littéraires*,
6 May 1939.

18. Raitt, p. 115. Reminiscences of these trips are found in "Souvenir" (*OC*, XI, 96–98) and "Augusta Holmès" (*OC*, XI, 106–13).

19. On Villiers and the Commune, see articles by Jacques-Henry Bornecque (*Mercure de France*, August 1953) and Drougard (*Mercure de France*, March 1958).

20. See Raitt, pp. 212–13.

21. See Drougard, "L'Erudition de Villiers de l'Isle-Adam," *Mercure de France*, CCXV (October 1929), 111–12.

22. See Meulen, *L'Idéalisme de Villiers de l'Isle-Adam* (Amsterdam: H. J. Paris, 1925), pp. 36–39.

23. Raitt, p. 221.

24. *Ibid.*, p. 224.

25. *Ibid.*, p. 189.

26. For further details, see Raitt, p. 211.

27. J.-K. Huysmans, *A Rebours* (Paris: Editions Fasquelle, 1968), p. 239.

28. Rodolphe Palgen, *Villiers de l'Isle-Adam: auteur dramatique* (Paris: Honoré Champion, 1925), p. 11.

29. *Ibid.*, p. 8; Lanfredini, pp. 27–28.

30. See, for example, Raitt, p. 73.

31. Michelet (pp. 53–54) suggests another source.

32. For further details, see Palgen, p. 14.

33. For further analysis, see Palgen, pp. 15, 17; Daireaux, pp. 328–29.

34. See Palgen, p. 19.

35. See *ibid.*, pp. 27–28.

36. *LP*, p. 36.

37. The work is found in *Reliques*, ed. P.-G. Castex (Paris; Corti, 1954), p. 64.

38. Auriant, "Petite Histoire littéraire," *Mercure de France*, 15 September 1938, p. 743.

39. The prose poem is reprinted in Auriant's article, *ibid.*, p. 742. On Armida, see A. B. Giamatti, *The Earthly Paradise and the Renaissance Epic* (Princeton: Princeton University Press, 1966), pp. 179–210.

40. Raitt, p. 154.

41. This phenomenon had not been scientifically established when Villiers wrote "Claire Lenoir." According to Drougard, Villiers made a "scientific anticipation in the manner of Jules Verne" (II, 82). But it is possible that he relied on an article in *Publicateur des Côtes-du-Nord*, 26 September 1863. See *Corr*, I, 85.

42. In the 1887 version, Claire is no longer a Christian Hegelian but simply a Christian; Césaire remains an atheistic Hegelian.

43. The division into chapters will disappear in the 1883 version of "L'Intersigne."

44. Raitt, pp. 89–92.
45. For a further discussion of Poe's influence, see Raitt, pp. 85–100; Droug, II, 24–27, 138–39, 153–56.
46. Cf. Daireaux, p. 324; André Lebois, *Villiers de l'Isle-Adam* (Neuchâtel: Messeiller, 1952), pp. 78–79; Vincent O'Sullivan, "The Tales and Stories of Villiers de l'Isle-Adam," *Dublin Magazine* (April-June 1940), pp. 25–34.
47. For a further discussion of sources, see Droug, II, 54–76, 123–40.
48. The 1883 version of "L'Intersigne" reads: "We naturally spoke of God. / I was tired: I listened without answering. / 'To conclude,' Maucombe said to me in getting up, 'We are here to bear witness' " (Droug, I, 178).
49. Edward Daniel Hayes, "Two Satirists of the Apocalypse" (Dissertation, University of South Carolina 1971), p. 101.
50. Cf. Castex, in *CC*, p. xxxiii; Chupeau, in *Contes et récits*, p. 24; Daireaux, pp. 383–85, 400; Lebois, pp. 153–54; Raitt, p. 193.
51. Droug, II, 158. See pp. 157–204 of this volume for a discussion of the other sources used by Villiers in composing the various versions of "Azraël."
52. Lanfredini, p. 117.
53. Droug, II, 200.
54. Droug, II, 168.
55. "Thus is sleeping, under the solemnity of the centuries, with the nearby noises of the torrents, the citadel of God, Zion the Predestined."
56. Droug, II, 259.

Chapter Three

1. Pontavice, pp. 84–85.
2. Cf. Raitt, pp. 16–17; P.–G. Castex places it a bit earlier. See "La Tentation," *Revue d'Histoire Littéraire de la France*, 56 (January-March 1956), pp. 1–29.
3. *LP*, 17–19.
4. Castex and Raitt disagree; they think Villiers went to Nantes to work on *Le Nouveau Monde* and *L'Evasion*. See *LP*, 17, n. 17.
5. Max Prinet writes: "The genealogy appears solidly established from Jérôme de Villiers, Parisian attorney, who died toward the end of 1676; but before him, the chain is broken" ("Les Ancêtres parisiens de Villiers de l'Isle-Adam," *Mercure de France*, CCV [1928], 587). Cf. in the same article, pp. 591–92; Drougard, "Villiers de l'Isle-Adam: défenseur de son nom," *Annales de Bretagne*, LXII, 1 (1955), 69.
6. Drougard, "Villiers de l'Isle-Adam: défenseur de son nom," p. 255.
7. *LP*, 30.
8. *Ibid.*, p. 32, n. 32.
9. Pontavice, pp. 135–42.
10. *Ibid.*, p. 142.

11. These tales are reprinted in *OC*, XI, 234–63. "Lady Hamilton," whose heroine already figured in *Morgane*, is derived from Gautier's *Souvenirs d'une favorite*. In 1880, Villiers would publish another story on Isabeau, this one more imaginative. "Hypermnestra" is long and slow moving.

12. Remy de Gourmont claims that "he was a boxing coach in a gymnasium" *(Promenades littéraires*, 2ᵉ série [Paris: Mercure de France, 1906], p. 32). Henri de Régnier claims that Villiers for a time served as an aid to a physician treating mental disorders *(Faces et profils* [Paris: Jacques Bernard, 1931], pp. 20–21). It may also be that Villiers earned money by giving piano lessons *(Corr,* I, 262).

13. Pontavice, p. 178.

14. *Ibid,* pp. 182–83.

15. *Ibid.,* p. 186.

16. *Ibid.,* p. 188.

17. *Ibid.,* pp. 188–201.

18. Cf. Raitt, p. 22; Rougemont, pp. 232–34.

19. Raitt, p. 22.

20. Palgen, pp. 43, 45.

21. *Ibid.,* pp. 41–48; Lanfredini, pp. 63–64; Daireaux, pp. 336–37.

22. "I don't know what they've done to me"; "The young bourgeois would have treated her like a dog, now that they are happy."

23. "I won't kill them"; "Let's see, not a question of that"; "[There's] only this door."

24. "It seems to me that it is now I am escaping."

25. Palgen, p. 44.

26. LP, 27.

27. For further details, see *LP,* 24–25.

28. See *The Dictionary of National Biography* (Oxford University Press, 1921–1922), vol. III; Ewen Butler, *The Cecils* (London: Frederick Muller, 1964).

29. Ironically, transformation of the historical past was the very thing he found so objectionable in the play *Perrinet Leclerc,* where his ancestor was portrayed as a traitor.

30. Raitt, pp. 126–29.

31. Michelet, p. 57. René de Berval, on the other hand, is more complimentary. See "Hommage à Villiers de l'Isle-Adam," *Mercure de France* (1 September 1938), p. 320.

32. At the beginning of Act II, Mistress Andrews has just arrived in Yorktown from Swinmore, where Act I takes place. About three months *(OC,* VII, 162), the time necessary to cross the Atlantic in the eighteenth century, has elapsed. To inform the audience of the change in time and place, Villiers clumsily has Moscone express disbelief in the arrival: "I do

not understand anything any more, Madame Edith! Indeed! the crossing is done; we are here! In America! In Yorktown! A few hours from your home" (139). Then, as if to orient those not acquainted with the American landscape, he has Moscone elaborate: "It is Yorktown, I tell you! We are several leagues from Mount Vernon, it is very close to Fredericksburg" (141).

33. For example, Mistress Andrews proclaims her all-sacrificing and all-consuming love for Stephen ("To live near him, hardly his friend, alas! lost in a village of the New World, I have left, sacrificed, forgotten the rest of the earth, without regrets and forever. . . . He is my family, he is earth and country!" [122]). The appearance of the bloody hand of Ralph Evandale is straight from a melodrama (320).

34. Henri de Vaudreuil just happens to belong to a branch of Ruth's family that "fled to France during the religious wars" (104). Moscone conveniently meets Bob Upfill whom he "left under a table, one autumn midnight, three years ago, in a bar in the city of London" (151–52), in Yorktown at the beginning of Act II. Mistress Andrews happens to arrive in Yorktown minutes before Ruth and Stephen's boat appears. It seems a bit unbelievable, too, that both Ruth and Stephen should have at different times saved Dahu's life.

35. For a further discussion of satire, see Gilbert Highet, *The Anatomy of Satire* (Princeton: Princeton University Press, 1962), especially pp. 21–22.

36. *Ibid.*, pp. 13–14, see especially p. 14.

37. This filiation is underlined by Villiers' cross-references. He alludes to the engineer of "La Découverte de M. Grave" in "La Machine à gloire" (*CC*, 61) and to Grave's discovery and Bottom's glory machine in "Le Traitment du Dr Tristan Chavassus" (265).

38. Ironically, in developing these machines, Villiers anticipates some actual future inventions. The projection of slogans onto the sky, described in "La Découverte de M. Grave," anticipates modern advertising. The "Machine à gloire" anticipates recorded applause.

39. *Claire Lenoir*, tr., Arthur Symons (New York: Boni, 1925), p. xxvi.

40. In the 1883 version, he falls into the drum and vanishes (*CC*, 147).

41. P–G. Castex, *Le Conte fantastique en France* (Paris: José Corti, 1951), p. 360.

42. Raitt, p. 194.

43. Chupeau, in *Contes et récits*, p. 61; Raitt, p. 194.

44. Raitt, p. 258.

45. See Raitt, p. 256; Peter Bürgisser, *La Double Illusion de l'or et de l'amour* (Berne: Herbert Lang, 1969), p. 88. For another interpretation of the deaf woman's remarks, see Deborah Conyngham, *Le Silence éloquent* (Paris: José Corti, 1975), pp. 80–82.

46. Unlike "El Desdichado" and the two 1878 versions of "Souvenirs

occultes," Villiers relates the 1883 version of the tale through an intermediary character. The first line reads: "I, last Gael, am descended, he said to me, from a family of Celts" (*CC*, 276).

47. For further development, see *CC*, 137, 140, notes d and e.

48. "The dusty slope of the mountain reddened from the cold fires . . .";
"Suddenly, one of them, svelte and pale, approached the rampart"; "A kind of holy anger made him forget his duties."

49. "Nevertheless, this multitude with harsh mouths imposed silence on itself because of the virgins."

50. "The catapults whirred, sending volleys of stones whose impact sounded after a thousand whizzes. . . ."

51. Jean–Paul Gourevitch, *Villiers de l'Isle-Adam* (Paris: Editions Pierre Seghers, 1971), p. 37.

52. See Raitt, pp. 235–36.

53. For a further development of sources, see Drougard, "L'Art de Villiers de l'Isle-Adam," *La Grande Revue*, 142 (July 1933), 100–12; Léon Lemonnier, "L'Influence d'Edgar Poe sur Villiers de l'Isle-Adam," *Mercure de France*, CCXLVI (15 September 1933), 604–19; Raitt, pp. 94–95.

Chapter Four

1. A. W. Raitt, "The Last Days of Villiers de l'Isle-Adam," *French Studies*, 8 (July 1954), 233.

2. Cf. Raitt, *Villiers de l'Isle-Adam*, pp. 30–31, 39.

3. In a letter dated 22 August 1881, Villiers appears indifferent to the defeat: "Without deluding myself about the outcome of the race, I agreed [to run] out of devotion and duty—being of those, moreover, who, indifferent by tradition to easy victories, never resist the honor of a battle where defeat is certain" (*Corr*, II, 10). In truth, this defeat probably confirmed his hostility to democratic institutions.

4. Raitt, *Villiers de l'Isle-Adam*, p. 31.

5. Remy de Gourmont, *Promenades littéraires*, 4ᵉ série (Paris: Mercure, 1912), p. 78.

6. *Le Figaro*, 20 February 1883, p. 3.

7. Raitt, *Villiers de l'Isle-Adam*, p. 55. See Villiers' answer to an unfavorable critic (*OC*, XI, 160–65).

8. Raitt, "Last Days," p. 235.

9. See *Corr*, I, 56–60, 145, 151–52, II, 13, 19–20.

10. See Gourmont, *Promenades littéraires*, 2ᵉ série, p. 10; Lanfredini, p. 73, 160; Raitt, *Villiers de l'Isle-Adam*, p. 200. For a detailed discussion of Villiers and religion, see Raitt, *Villiers de l'Isle-Adam*, pp. 74–75; Daireaux, pp. 257–58.

11. Raitt, "Last Days," p. 238.

12. See, for example, Michelet, p. 13.

13. For additional information on these revisions, see *CC*, 435–91; Droug, I, 31–240; II, 207-48; as well as the relevant portions of Chapters 2 and 3.

14. Chupeau, in *Contes et récits*, p. 237.

15. See *CC*, 81–90, notes.

16. On the choice of the title, see *CC*, introduction, pp. xvi–xvii.

17. L. Seylaz, *Edgar Poe et les premiers symbolistes français* (Lausanne: La Concorde, 1923), pp. 125–26. For refutation, see Raitt, *Villiers de l'Isle-Adam*, p. 96.

18. Raitt, *Villiers de l'Isle-Adam, p. 196.*

19. Pontavice, pp. 160–64; Rougemont, p. 266. For refutation, see Chupeau, in *Contes et récits*, p. 139.

20. See, for example, Lebois, p. 151; Jean-Aubry, pp. 65–66.

21. Under the title *L'Eve nouvelle*, Book One was published in *Le Gaulois* between 4 September 1880 and 18 September 1880. All but three chapters was completed in 1879–1880 and, under the same title, published in *L'Etoile française* from 15 December 1880 to 4 February 1881.

22. See Conyngham, pp. 10–12.

23. See *Corr*, I, 263: "There are certain analyses of the bourgeois entity that will be able to make you exult [. . .]. But there are also other things. . . . It is complicated."

24. Conyngham, p. 64.

25. Raitt, *Villiers de l'Isle-Adam*, p. 250.

26. See also *OC*, I, 384.

27. See Conyngham, pp. 134–36; Raitt, *Villiers de l'Isle-Adam*, p. 194, 250.

28. Raitt, *Villiers de l'Isle-Adam*, p. 179.

29. Chupeau, in *Contes et récits*, p. 145.

30. See Conyngham, pp. 64, 113–14, 123.

31. See Raitt, *Villiers de l'Isle-Adam*, pp. 196–200. This critic points out Villiers' early fascination with the legend and claims *L'Eve future* is Villiers' *Faust*.

32. Raitt, *Villiers de l'Isle-Adam*, p. 199.

33. At least one other critic sees affinities between Villiers and the two protagonists. See Pierre Biessy, *Etude médico-psychologique* (Valence: Charpin & Reyne, 1923), p. 24.

34. Raitt, *Villiers de l'Isle-Adam*, pp. 197–200.

35. See Conyngham, pp. 19–23, 122–24.

36. Lebois, p. 154.

37. "Suddenly, one heard the deafened murmurings of the timbrels mixed with clashes of arms and chains—and, broken by the sonorous shocks of the cymbals."

38. For further details, see Daireaux, pp. 391–400; some of his criticisms, however, may be a bit harsh.

39. For further details, see Droug, II, 210–11, 221–27, and Raitt, *Villiers de l'Isle Adam*, pp. 239–43.
40. See Droug, II, 226.
41. See *CC*, pp. 313, 338, 345, 350, 358.
42. See Pierre Reboul, "Autour d'un conte de Villiers de l'Isle-Adam," *Revue d'Histoire Littéraire de la France*, 49 (July-September 1949), 235–45.

Chapter Five

1. Cf. Raitt, *Villiers de l'Isle-Adam*, pp. 272–73.
2. Cf. E. Drougard, "Les *Histoires souveraines* de Villiers de l'Isle-Adam," *Annales de Bretagne*, LV (1948), 69–107.
3. Raitt, *Villiers de l'Isle-Adam*, pp. 36–39.
4. Edmond Jaloux, "Le Centenaire de Villiers de l'Isle-Adam," *Le Temps*, 12 August 1938, p. 3.
5. A. W. Raitt, "Etat présent des études sur Villiers de l'Isle-Adam," *L'Information littéraire* (January-February 1956), p. 6.
6. The few other critical works Villiers wrote include "La Légende moderne" (*OC*, VI, 169–81), "Sur une pièce d'Emile Augier" (*OC*, XI, 231–33), and the following not collected in the *Oeuvres complètes:* an essay on Catulle Mendès' *Philoméla* (*Revue nouvelle*, 1 December 1863); summaries of *Das Rheingold* (*L'Universelle*, 21 September 1869) and *Lohengrin* (*Le Citoyen*, 6 April 1870); notice of the Munich Exposition (reproduced in *Nouvelles littéraires*, 27 July 1939); analysis of Judith Gautier's *Dragon impérial* (reproduced in *Mercure de France*, 1 November 1939).
7. Cf. Raitt, *Villiers de l'Isle-Adam*, p. 46.
8. John Milton, *Paradise Lost* (Garden City, N. Y.: Doubleday, 1969), III, i.
9. Gourmont, *Promenades littéraires*, 2ᵉ série (Paris: Mercure de France, 1913), pp. 15–16.
10. Pontavice (p. 34) states that Villiers conceived *Axël* in 1855. It seems more probable that the idea for a drama with a philosophic core came not earlier than 1862. See Drougard, "L'"Axël de Villiers de l'Isle-Adam," pp. 510–14, 518; Raitt, *Villiers de l'Isle-Adam*, p. 205.
11. Palgen (p. 49), Daireaux (p. 424), and Rougemont (p. 154) claim that the entire play was complete by 1872. Even if it were, there is no guarantee that it was like the version we have today. See Drougard, "l' 'Axël,' " pp. 520–21. On performing *Axël*, see Raitt, *Villiers de l'Isle-Adam*, pp. 55–57.
12. Drougard, "Le Vrai Sens d' 'Axël,' " *La Grande Revue*, 135 (April 1931), 276.
13. Drougard, "Les Sources d' 'Axël,' " *Revue d'Histoire Littéraire de la France*, 43 (1936), 554.
14. "Courage! Alone, the last [heiress] blazes forth"; "Bejeweled, I hope to rise higher."

15. Cf. *Les Reliques*, pp. 33–36.

16. Remy de Gourmont, "Notes sur Villiers de l'Isle-Adam," *Mercure de France* (August 1890), p. 91.

17. Drougard, "Le Vrai Sens d' 'Axël,' " pp. 282–83.

18. The play may have at one time consisted of three parts. See Drougard, "L' 'Axël,' " p. 539.

19. Arthur Symons, *The Symbolist Movement in Literature* (New York: Dutton, 1911), p. 45.

20. Cf. Drougard, "Les Sources d' 'Axël,' " p. 558–59; Palgen, pp. 54, 57–60, 62–63, 89.

21. Palgen, pp. 53, 59, 61, 65.

22. Edmund Wilson, *Axel's Castle* (New York: Scribner's 1931), p. 259.

Conclusion

1. For technical vocabulary, see Conyngham, pp. 10–11.

2. George Moore, *Memoirs of My Dead Life* (New York: Appleton, 1907), p. 88.

3. Notably Raitt in his *Villiers de l'Isle-Adam et le mouvement symboliste* and Edmund Wilson in *Axel's Castle*.

4. Raitt, *Villiers de l'Isle-Adam*, pp. 261–62.

5. *Ibid*, p. 59.

6. Rougemont, p. 109.

7. Michelet, p. 63.

8. H. F. Carlill, "Villiers de l'Isle-Adam," *Literature*, V (5 August 1899), 131.

Selected Bibliography

PRIMARY SOURCES

1. First Editions:

Deux Essais de poésie. Paris: L. Tinterlin, 1858.
Premières Poésies. Lyons: N. Scheuring, 1859.
Isis. Paris: E. Dentu, 1862.
Elën. Paris: Louis Davyl, 1865.
Morgane. Saint-Brieuc: Guyon Francisque, 1866.
La Révolte. Paris: Alphonse Lemerre, 1870.
Le Nouveau Monde. Paris: Richard et Cie, 1880.
Contes cruels. Paris: Calmann-Lévy, 1883.
L'Eve future. Paris: M. de Brunhoff, 1886.
Akëdysséril. Paris: M. de Brunhoff, 1886.
L'Amour suprême. Paris: M. de Brunhoff, 1886.
Tribulat Bonhomet. Paris: Tresse & Stock, 1887.
Histoires insolites. Paris: Quantin, 1888.
Nouveaux Contes cruels. Paris: Librairie illustrée, 1888.
Axël. Paris: Quantin, 1890.
Chez les passants. Paris: Comptoir d'édition, 1890.
L'Evasion. Paris: Tresse & Stock, 1891.
Propos d'Au-delà (with *Nouveaux Contes cruels*). Paris: Calmann-Lévy, 1893.

2. Important Modern Editions:

Axël. Ed., Pierre Mariel. Paris: La Colombe, 1960. Includes introduction and notes.
Contes cruels, Nouveaux Contes cruels. Ed., P.-G. Castex. Paris: Garnier, 1968. Contains informative notes and appendix of variants.
Contes et récits. Ed., Jacques Chupeau. Paris: Bordas, 1970. Selection of works with interesting introduction and notes. Chronology has some errors.
Correspondance générale. Ed., Joseph Bollery. Paris: Mercure de France,

159

1962, 2 vols. Gathers Villiers' letters and includes those written to him. Commentary is most helpful.

L'Eve future. Ed., J. Bollery and P.-G. Castex. Paris: Le Club du meilleur livre, 1957. Critical introduction; illustrations by Jacques Noël.

Oeuvres. Ed., Jacques-Henry Bornecque. Paris: Le Club français, 1957. Contains important introductory essay.

Oeuvres complètes. Paris: Mercure de France, 1914–1931. 11 vols. Standard French text cited.

Le Prétendant. Ed., P.-G. Castex and A. W. Raitt. Paris: José Corti, 1965. The definitive reworking of *Morgane,* heretofore unpublished, Thorough and scholarly introduction.

Tribulat Bonhomet. Ed., P.-G. Castex and J.-M. Bellefroid. Paris: José Corti. 1967.

Les Trois Premiers Contes. Ed., E. Drougard. Paris: Les Belles Lettres, 1931. 2 vols. Complete and very informative critical edition of "Claire Lenoir," "L'Intersigne," and "L'Annonciateur."

Reliques. Ed., P.-G. Castex. Paris: José Corti, 1954. Fragments left behind after Villiers' death.

3. Translations:

Axël. Trans., H.P.R. Finberg. London: Jarolds, 1925. Includes preface by W. B. Yeats.

Axël. Trans., June Guicharnaud. Englewoods Cliffs, N.J.: Prentice-Hall, 1970.

Axël. Trans., Marilyn Gaddis Rose. Dublin: Dolmen Press, 1970. Reprints preface by W.B. Yeats.

Claire Lenoir. Trans., Arthur Symons. New York: Boni, 1925.

Cruel Tales. Trans., Robert Baldick. London: Oxford University Press, 1963.

The Revolt, The Escape. Trans., Theresa Barclay. London: Duckworth, 1910.

SECONDARY SOURCES

1. General Works:

CLERGET, FERNAND. *Villiers de l'Isle-Adam.* Paris: Michaud, 1913. Interesting introduction to Villiers.

DAIREAUX, MAX. *Villiers de l'Isle-Adam.* Paris: Desclée de Brouwer, 1936. Well-documented biography with study of works.

LEBOIS, ANDRE. *Villiers de l'Isle-Adam.* Neuchâtel: Messeiller, 1952. Cursory analysis of works, ideas, techniques. At times impressionistic.

MICHELET, VICTOR-EMILE. *Villiers de l'Isle-Adam.* Paris: Durville, 1910. Should be supplemented with Daireaux and Rougemont.

PONTAVICE DE HEUSSEY, ROBERT DU. *Villiers de l'Isle-Adam.* Trans., Mary

Loyd. New York: Dodd, Mead, 1894. Very readable but contains numerous errors.

ROUGEMONT, E. DE. *Villiers de l'Isle-Adam*. Paris: Mercure de France, 1910. Outdated in some ways, but still, along with Daireaux's study, the best general work.

2. Biographical Studies:

BOLLERY, JOSEPH. "Documents biographiques inédits." *Revue d'Histoire Littéraire de la France*, 56 (1956), 30–49. On Villiers' ties to Brittany.

DROUGARD, E. "Villiers de l'Isle-Adam: défenseur de son nom." *Annales de Bretagne*, LXII (1955), 62–117, 237–80. Study of Villiers' genealogy.

JEAN-AUBRY, G. *Une Amitié exemplaire*. Paris: Mercure de France, 1942. Villiers' friendship with Mallarmé. Enjoyable reading.

PRINET, MAX. "Les Ancêtres parisiens de Villiers de l'Isle-Adam." *Mercure de France*, CCV (1928), 586–593. Another study of Villiers' genealogy.

RAITT, A. W. "The Last Days of Villiers de l'Isle-Adam." *French Studies*, 8 (1954), 233–49. Well documented and well written.

TIERCELIN, LOUIS. "Villiers de l'Isle-Adam." *La Nouvelle Revue*, nouvelle série, 6 (1900), 26–45. Investigates Villiers' youth, relying on unpublished documents.

3. Critical Studies:

BÜRGISSER, PETER. *La Double Illusion de l'or et de l'amour*. Berne: Herbert Lang, 1969. Gold and love as they relate to Villiers' works, especially *Axël*. Technical psychological vocabulary.

CASTEX, P.-G., and J. BOLLERY. *Contes cruels: etude historique et littéraire*. Paris: José Corti, 1956. Indispensable guide to the tales.

CONYNGHAM, DEBORAH. *Le Silence éloquent*. Paris: José Corti, 1975. Tries to view *L'Eve future* as an integrated piece of literature. Interesting and helpful.

DROUGARD, E. "L 'Axël' de Villiers de l'Isle-Adam." *Revue d'Histoire Littéraire 'de la France*, 42 (1935), 509–46. This and the following articles by Drougard are clear, well documented, and immensely useful.

———. "L'Erudition deVilliers de l'Isle-Adam." *Mercure de France*, CCXV (1929), 97–112.

———. "Les Sources d' 'Axël.' " *Revue d'Histoire Littéraire de la France* 43 (1936), 551–67.

———. "Le Vrai Sens d' 'Axël.' " *La Grande Revue*, 135 (1931), 262–84.

LANFREDINI, DINA. *Villiers de l'Isle-Adam*. Florence: Felice Le Monnier, 1940. Cursory but sound evaluation of the works.

LEMONNIER, LEON. "L'Influence d'Edgar Poe sur Villiers de L'Isle-Adam." *Mercure de France*, CCXLVI (1933), 604–19. Outlines themes and techniques Villiers may have borrowed from the American.

PALGEN, RODOLPHE. *Villiers de l'Isle-Adam: auteur dramatique*. Paris:

Champion, 1925. Study of Villiers as playwright. Omits discussion of *Le Nouveau Monde*. Overly critical of Villiers' early plays.

RAITT, A. W. *Villiers de l'Isle-Adam et le mouvement symboliste*. Paris: José Corti, 1965. A monumental work: scholarly, well-documented, penetrating insights.

WILSON, EDMUND. *Axel's Castle*. New York: Scribner's 1943. Views Axël as the first great embodiment of a whole family of symbolic characters in modern literature.

Index

163

Georges, Alexandre, 100
Gesamtkunstwerk, 81, 141
Ghys, Henry, 100
Gil Blas, Le, 101, 103
Girardin, Emile de, 38, 106
Goethe, Johann Wolfgang von, 86, 111,
   113, 140
Gounod, Charles: *Faust*, 113
Gourevitch, Jean-Paul, 97
Gourmont, Remy de, 100, 126, 127, 138
Guéranger, Dom, 20–21, 35, 41

Hegel, Friedrich, 19, 22, 38, 41, 42, 43,
   54, 60, 97–98, 105, 137, 143
Hegelianism. *See* Hegel
Heredia, José-Maria de, 60
Heredia, Severiano de, 100
Herpent, Godefroy d' (Jules de Cler-
   ville), 65–66
Holmès, Augusta, 38, 128
Hugo, Victor, 20, 24, 25, 70, 140
Huysmans, Joris-Karl, 43, 101, 102,
   103, 105, 118, 126, 133, 138

Ibsen, Henrik: *A Doll's House*, 51
Ideal, theme of, 25, 33, 41–42, 44–45,
   50, 97, 110, 130, 131
Illusionism, 91, 98, 105, 111–112, 116,
   131, 136–137, 142, 143
Influence on Symbolists, 36, 42, 144,
   158n3
Irony, 41, 46, 48, 51, 52, 73, 81, 86, 87,
   89, 90, 94, 107, 122

Jesus Christ, 32, 33, 61, 136–37
Jeune France, La, 102, 133
Juan, Don, 24–25, 26–27, 28–29

Kérinou, Marie-Félix Daniel de (maternal great-aunt), 17, 18, 21, 22, 23, 35,
   36, 41, 63, 102
Kraemer, Alexis von, 127

Lamartine, Alphonse, 24, 25, 26
Lanfredini, Dina, 60
Latin, knowledge of, 19, 147n8

Le Menant des Chesnais, Amédée, 19,
   20–21, 22, 28, 41
Lemercier de Neuville, Louis, 20, 22
Lévi, Eliphas: *Dogme et rituel de la
   haute magie*, 19, 38, 56, 57, 91, 111
Liberté, La, 38
Liszt, Franz, 40
Lockroy, Edouard. *See* Bourgeois
Love, theme of, 29, 30–32, 42, 43, 45,
   46, 53, 71, 74–75, 85, 89, 91–92, 107,
   111, 116–17, 121, 122, 130, 131, 137
Lune, La, 38

Maeterlinck, Maurice, 144
Magdalene, Mary, 32, 33, 42
Mallarmé, Stéphane, 36, 37, 38, 40, 41,
   42, 58, 64, 99, 101, 102, 104, 105, 109,
   126, 127, 133
Marras, Jean, 36, 42, 105, 115
Maupassant, Guy de, 144
Mendès, Catulle, 19, 35, 38, 39–40
Mercure de France, 126
Mérimée, Prosper, 144
Michaëlis, Theodore, 64, 66
Michelet, Victor-Emile, 24
Milton, John, 131–33
Monnier, Henri, 57
Moore, George, 143, 144
Music, 19, 39, 40, 46, 49, 52, 68, 79–80,
   81, 88, 100, 140–41
Musset, Alfred de, 24, 25, 26, 46

Napoleon III, 36, 40, 108
Nerval, Gérard de, 52

Occultism, 38, 41, 42, 54, 60, 91, 98,
   105, 112, 136, 137, 143

Palgen, Rodolphe, 69, 70, 71
Parnasse contemporain, Le, 37, 60
Parnassian influence, 60
Pierre, Emile: *Le Rêve d'aimer*, 128
Poe, Edgar Allan, 22, 38, 41, 54, 56, 59,
   97, 101, 104, 111, 124–25, 144
Pontavice de Heussey, Hyacinthe du,
   22, 23, 35, 42
Pontavice de Heussey, Robert du, 36,
   63, 66, 67–68, 111, 127

Raitt, A. W., 53, 74, 113, 128, 129
Régnier, Henri de, 37
Renaissance littéraire et artistique, La, 63, 133
Revue contemporaine, La, 102
Revue des Lettres et des Arts, La, 23, 38, 56
Revue fantaisiste, La, 35, 37, 60
Revue illustrée, La, 104
Revue libre, La, 103
Revue wagnerienne, La, 117
Rimbaud, Arthur, 99
Robin, Dr. Albert, 103, 104
Rodenbach, Georges, 127
Romantic influence, 24–27, 43, 50
Rougemont, E. de, 24, 127

Salisbury, Lord Cecil Marquis of, 104
Satire, 51, 58, 82–90, 95, 96, 97, 106–107, 109, 111, 118–19, 122–23, 133, 143
Seer, theme of, 42, 59, 60, 116, 132, 144
Sherring, Matthew Atmore: *The Sacred City of the Hindus*, 117
Soulary, Joséphin, 22, 37
Succès, Le, 102
Symbolist movement, 127, 128, 130, 144; *See also* Influence on Symbolists

Tiercelin, Louis, 19, 21
Torquemada, Tomas de, 121–22, 140
Tribun du peuple, Le, 41

Véra, Auguste: *Introduction à la philosophie de Hegel*, 42, 57
Verlaine, Paul, 24, 38, 99, 101, 104, 127
Veuillot, Louis, 36
Vie moderne, La, 102
Vie pour rire, La, 103
Vigny, Alfred de, 24, 25
Villard, Nina de, 38, 102
Villiers de l'Isle-Adam, Jean-Jérôme de (paternal grandfather), 52
Villiers de l'Isle-Adam, Jean-Marie Mathias Philippe Auguste de: ancestors, 17; birth, 17; Commune, 41;

death, 106, 126; early sojourns in Paris, 20; early romances, 20; eclipse of fame after death, 127; education, 18–19; family's move to Paris, 21–22; Franco-Prussian War, 40; growing celebrity, 99–101; illnesses, 102–103, 103–104; liaison with Louise Dyonnet, 35–37; liaison with Marie Dantine, 99; marriage plans, 38, 64, 67; meets Baudelaire, 22; meets Mallarmé, 36; parental influences, 18; *Perrinet Leclerc* affair, 65; posthumous revival, 127–28; retreats at Solesmes, 35–36; solitary childhood, 19; starts writing short stories, 38; stay in Montfort-sur-Meu, 20–21; supposed candidacy for the Greek throne, 36; trip to Belgium, 103–104; trip to Dieppe, 104; trip to London, 64; trips to Germany, 39–40; turns to prose, 22

WORKS–DRAMA:
Axël, 19, 42, 63, 69, 102, 106, 126, 127, 128, *133–42*, 143, 144
Elën, 37, 42, *44–46*, 48, 49, 52, 79, 81, 127, 143
Evasion, L', 63, *69–71*, 82, 102, 103, 129
Morgane (Le Prétendant), 19, 20, 37, 42, *46–50*, 52, 64, 66, *71–75*, 79, _127, 128
Nouveau Monde, Le, 19, 64, 66, 69, *75–82*, 100, 101, 104, 133, 141, 144, 153n32, 154n33, 154n34
Prétendant, Le (Morgane), 64, 65–66, 69, *71–75*, 79, 82, 116, 128, 141, 143, 144
Révolte, La, 39–40, *50–52*, 63, 80, 127, 130, 133, 141, 143
Tentation, La, 63

WORKS–NOVELS:
Eve future, L', 35, 67, 100, 102, *109–15*, 116, 127, 131, 137, 138, 142, 143, 144, 156n21
Isis, 19, 22, 35, *41–44*, 92, 116, 127, 141, 143, 144

WORKS–POETRY:
Deux Essais de poésie, 20, 21, 23